Have Work Will Travel

Have Work Will Travel
Lessons of a Wanderer

Elizabeth Scott

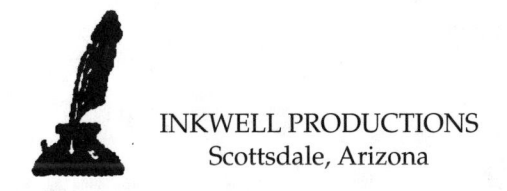

INKWELL PRODUCTIONS
Scottsdale, Arizona

Copyright © 2002 by Elizabeth Ann Scott
First printing June 2002
All rights reserved. No part of this book may be reproduced or utilized in any form or by any means, electronic or mechanical, including photocopying, recording, or by any information storage and retrieval system, without permission in writing from the publisher.
ISBN 0-9718155-6-9
Library of Congress: 2002107511

Published by:
Inkwell Productions
3370 North Hayden Road #123-276
Scottsdale, AZ 85251
Telephone (480) 315-9636
Fax (480) 315-9641
Toll-free: (888) 324-BOOK (2665)
Website www.inkwellproductions.com
E-Mail info@inkwellproductions.com

Credits:
Editor: Patricia Turpin
Cover Design: Paul Klissas, V-Space Design
Typesetting: Madalyn Johnson, Type 'N Graphics
Manufactured in the United States of America

Acknowledgements

A year ago, my good friend Kathi Sheehan visited me in Sun Valley, Idaho. I relayed stories to her of people asking how I took my work with me to such wonderful places. She encouraged me to write a book about it, and Kathi has not wavered in her support since that day. I thank Kathi for the inspiration and wisdom she has shared with me.

My writing sojourn brought me to Leslie Buck, a fellow writer who has become a dear friend. Leslie was magnanimous in her encouragement and in her introduction to Nick Ligidakis, publisher at Inkwell Productions. Nick nourished my idea when confidence waned. His coaching fed my simple concept until it grew into a story with depth and soul.

None of this could have happened without John Reely. He has challenged me to be my best in every way. As master of a rare balance between work and play, family and friends, compassion and iron will, he is an example to admire. His support of this endeavor has been endless. My love and appreciation are endless, too.

I owe a debt of gratitude to Leslie Thomas, friend and business associate. As I took work on the road, she persevered through trials and tribulations. We went back and forth, trying systems that failed while she placated our clients. The kinks are out now, but it was a test of patience. Leslie saw my vision and stayed with me all the way.

One of the best real-life models I know for a "have work will travel" life is Sandee Harvey. In our joint escapades, she exemplifies creativity, grace and humor. I appreciate her example and her thoughts as they were incorporated into this book.

I thank Linda Zanides, my PR whiz and pal, for the generosity of her time and interest in this project. I admire Linda's insight and upbeat inspiration.

Katy Howes, my friend of many years, gave me more than she probably knows. I respect her opinions, which helped me drive the book closer to my vision and boosted my confidence in its message. New friends and old have been supportive. After a brief acquaintance, author and newfound friend Deni Tidwell dove in with enthusiasm and contributed.

Thank God for good friends.

Last but hardly least are Mom and Dad, to whom I owe a lifetime of thanks. Their examples of discipline, integrity, hard work, and generosity instilled values in me that I'll always carry. I hope to pass them on to future generations of our family. Their confidence in me, for as long as I can remember, boosted my ability to try anything I choose in life. I believe I can do whatever I set my mind to, thanks to my parents.

Dedication

This book is dedicated to Tara Grace and her big brother Jaime. By the time you finish this book, you will understand why.

TABLE OF CONTENTS

An Invitation to Share a Journey

Prologue

Part 1
In Search of FULFILLMENT

Chapter 1	COPING	5
	Life, illness and death — assess the damage.	
Chapter 2	LUPUS	13
	Use minimal motion for maximum effect to survive.	
Chapter 3	FLASHBACKS	19
	Recall childhood memories to boost confidence and identify talents.	
Chapter 4	HEALING	29
	While rebuilding, be true to core values.	

Part II
Tapping Into CURIOSITY

Chapter 5   TRIAL AND ERROR   43
             "If at first you don't succeed, try, try again" as the
             old saying goes. Admire other lifestyles — try
             them on for size.

Chapter 6   FORMULATE THE DREAM   54
             Analyze personal strengths and weaknesses before
             launching.

Chapter 7   BE REALISTIC   60
             Apply honesty during self-assessment, before
             making major decisions.

Chapter 8   MONETARY PROS AND CONS   66
             Look at financial aspects of a "have work will
             travel" life.

Chapter 9   LIFESTYLE PROS AND CONS   80
             There are social issues to consider, plus the value
             of time.

Part III
Developing DISCIPLINE

Chapter 10   PUT THE DREAM INTO ACTION   96
             Acquire portable skills to take on the road.

Chapter 11   ROLL UP YOUR SLEEVES   102
             It's time to get started. Phones, computers, mail
             box service — which tools are essential and when.

Chapter 12　TAKE IT ON THE ROAD　　　　　　　　114
　　　　　　　Juggle transportation, lodging, and keep up the work flow.

Chapter 13　NUTS, BOLTS AND TOOLBOXES　　　123
　　　　　　　Transport all the tools of the trade and the toys.

Part IV
Divine SIMPLICITY

Chapter 14　REFINE AS YOU GO　　　　　　　　　139
　　　　　　　Efficiency, adaptability and thoughtfulness tame chaos on the road.

Chapter 15　THE CRITICAL CORNER　　　　　　　154
　　　　　　　Naming names — the good, the bad and the ugly among office product manufacturers and service providers.

Chapter 16　LEAP OVER THE PITFALLS　　　　　　167
　　　　　　　Bridge potential problems of combining work and play.

Chapter 17　ON THE ROAD AGAIN　　　　　　　　173
　　　　　　　"Have Work Will Travel" continues to be a life-expanding journey and an attainable one.

Addendum 1   180
     MONETARY SAVINGS AND COSTS, Work Sheet

Addendum II   185
     TIME-WASTERS IN THE WORKPLACE, Work Sheet

Addendum III   187
     GRAND TOTAL OF MONETARY SAVINGS, Work Sheet

Addendum IV   188
     BILLS TO PAY, List

Addendum V   189
     TRAVEL LIST, List

Addendum VI   191
     WORLD TRAVELER'S PACKING LIST, List

Addendum VII   194
     ORGANIZING A TRAVEL BRIEFCASE, List

Addendum VIII   196
     HOUSEGUEST ETIQUETTE, List

Addendum IX   199
     RESOURCES

Index

About the Author

Order Form

AN INVITATION TO SHARE A JOURNEY

Please join Elizabeth Scott as she tells of her journey from despair to soaring high in the sky.

Share her climb out of the depths of coping with catastrophic loss and disability. Then take pleasure as the story transforms — becomes less intense, more upbeat, and more energetic. The fun of a "have work will travel" life emerges.

Learn from the foibles of the author and her friends as they put together lives that combine work and play. Perhaps you'll see a bit of yourself in their situations.

We are beginning an armchair journey via this book. At times the story is sad. But we will travel through it to the other side.

We'll have some fun as we look at new ways that we can live our old lives.

PROLOGUE

If you wonder about the lives behind people that you see adventuring around the continent and the world — you are not alone. How do they support themselves? How do they afford such trips? How do they get time off to travel? Or, do they work while they travel? It's a lifestyle envied by many and mastered by only a few. Financial independence is not a requirement. I hope to demystify the process for you after we take a little side journey. We have some groundwork to lay.

I have not always had work that would travel. At times I had the *opposite* of a "have work will travel" life. I felt like a prisoner of circumstances beyond my control. The first section of this book tells of my past: an extreme contrast to my present life.

For many years, survival was all I could ask for myself. Anything like "have work will travel" was beyond comprehension. What I learned as I struggled eventually brought me to a level of fulfillment — completion — satisfying the basic needs of health, a home, family, and enough money for the necessities of life. Only then could I begin to dream.

We all must attain fulfillment before we can begin to work

toward our dreams. So I share my tactics, step by step, as I moved from survival to fulfillment. If you are facing serious personal challenges related to health, family, spirit or career — perhaps you can learn from my experiences. You *can* get there from here.

When you begin reading *Have Work Will Travel*, know that it moves beyond my personal story. I want to show how life changes for all of us. As we go from one passage to the next, each with a different feel, a different tone, the story transitions into a work-travel tale with a happy ending. There were lessons learned as I grew confident and self-accepting. At that point, I made better choices. As I made better choices, circumstances improved, which led to my current passage in life — work that challenges me, travel when I want it, a home life I appreciate, and love in abundance.

With such wealth in my life, there is much to share — including how I put together a life of "have work will travel." I tell how various people I know combine work and play on the road. You'll see them apply four essential elements to create the life they want: **Fulfillment** is the springboard; **curiosity** spurs them on to each unknown step; **discipline** keeps them on track; and **simplicity** adds the clarity they need along the way.

There are also stories about people I know who aspire to "have work will travel" but can't comprehend how to make it a reality. If you are in this category, this book is for you.

We are all travelers.

But the journey begins at home.

In Search of
Fulfillment

Elizabeth Scott

Fulfillment means satisfaction, accomplishment and completion according to Webster's Dictionary. Words are more easily said than done, though. Fulfillment was a long quest for me after a series of disastrous setbacks. Ten years it took, to merely satisfy core survival needs — physical health, a stable home, viable work, and spiritual and emotional health. Until that was accomplished, fulfillment was impossible. The first chapters tell how I dug out of a deep hole and completed lessons that took me beyond survival to a basic level of fulfillment. Only then could I up the ante and see how grand life could be. After that, lessons in "have work will travel" began.

Elizabeth Scott

-1-

COPING

Life, illness and death: Assess the damage —

I was so-o-o tired. Sleeping in. Sort of awake, but too wasted to roll over or even lift my hands. My arms were dead weight, limp at my side. Both eyelids sealed shut, like magnets refusing to budge. The sensation of sinking into the mattress was surreal — the center of the earth could just suck me in.

Through the thick fog in my head and the dizzy hum in my ears, I heard the phone ringing in the distance. I wavered. "Stay put. That's what answering machines are for. Oh-h-h, might be important." With eyes still closed, I lay still as a startled bunny, prickling ears straining to hear the message. Marge's tiny voice came through. It is important. I slid out of bed and scuttled to the phone to answer it before she hung up.

"Marge, it's been so long. How are you?"

"OK. How is your lupus? Are you doing all right?"

"About the same. Not very well energywise. That's why I haven't been up to see Tara."

"I have terrible news about Tara. Are you sitting down?"

My breathing froze. "Yes."

"She died this morning. We don't know yet what happened." Marge was steady and compassionate through the long pause at my end of the phone line. I emerged from the fog in my head and absorbed what she was telling me, still frozen in time.

"Oh God. Oh-h my God!" My lungs finally expelled the panic, expanding to let in the despair. The worst was now a reality. "I always knew this would happen. But oh-h-h-h God ... not now." I struggled to speak in between sobs, with my hand cupped over my face, huddled deep down in the chair. "I was going to call you today ... I wanted to see her ... this weekend. It's been so long! ... Oh, my God! ... What happened?"

"Nancy was getting the kids ready for school this morning. Tara started out fine. When Nancy went back to her she wasn't breathing. We think it was over quickly. She didn't suffer."

For some reason, my next thought was for Marge's assistant, Nancy. "Nancy must be so upset." Words gurgled through my runny nose and spastic sobs. "We knew this would happen someday ... Nancy shouldn't blame herself. She did a great job. I don't blame her ... Will you tell her?"

This was how I found out my eight-year-old beloved daughter was dead. Even though the past year I had lived in San Francisco and Tara in Santa Rosa, we were connected always. I never knew what it was like to wail, like an Israeli mother over her son's grave. I didn't know I had it in me. I did.

Marge and I continued to talk as I calmed down. We spoke about Tara, about life, about my illness, about Marge's role in our lives. I was drained, starting to go numb. I could barely talk. With Marge's care-giving experience, she was able to tell me what to do after we said "goodbye."

"OK. Keep your head," I told myself. "There are people to contact and decisions to be made." Numbness has its value.

Unlike most parents, I expected to outlive my daughter. Just not so soon. Not when I hadn't seen her in so long. Not now! Tara, who had suffered from day one. Tara, who never hurt a soul or had a mean thought in her life. Tara, who didn't deserve any of this. Tara, who in her humble way had shaped my life forever.

This was the third time I had gone through a death with Tara. So some of the shock had already been absorbed. The first death was when she was 13 months old. We were in the office of a respected pediatric neurologist in San Francisco. He diagnosed the cause of Tara's lethargy. He said Tara had been born with brain damage and was affected both physically and mentally. Her life would always be very limited.

That session in the doctor's office was the death of everything I had hoped for my daughter. Dead was any vision I had of seeing her first toddling steps. Dead was the dream of Tara traipsing off to birthday parties wearing frilly dresses. Never would she dance to the rock music with rhythms she felt to the bone. In the weeks that followed there were more mini-deaths of my hopes for my daughter. Each loss brought sadness, then comforting tears to fill my eyes and drain the sorrow.

One of those mini-deaths occurred shortly after the diagnosis. I sat in our cabin in the mountains, with Tara in my lap, watching TV news. They were interviewing Kennedy family members about the newly formed Special Olympics. It struck a raw chord and I started sobbing. Overwhelming sadness for Tara, my own frustration, and helplessness all vied for position and fed my tears. I cried hysterically as Tara bounced up and down on my lap in choppy rhythm to my sobs.

Thoughts from every corner raced through my hysteria. It dawned on me that Tara would be the recipient of special treatment all of her life. Then again, she might not even be capable of the Special Olympics. A flash of indignation followed as I thought, "How dare they patronize these kids! I don't want people patronizing Tara." I wouldn't normally think that way — but rambling thoughts and irrational opinions punctuated my life for weeks after that first death, the diagnosis, as I assessed and re-assessed our loss.

Tara's second death came when she was three years old. After two years of immersion in Tara's care regime including work with physical therapists, occupational therapists, special educators, and groups for disabled toddlers, I had to cry "uncle." It was time to place her in a home for the disabled. Even with full-time work on my part, her intelligence would never thrive. It would never even support her in basic mental reasoning. She would never effectively feed herself. She would never do much more than roll over (with a lot of cheering on my part and grunting on her part).

She was eager to please, even though her daily exercises were painful. Cerebral palsy resulted in tight muscles that would stiffen to permanent rigidity if left alone. Those muscles had to be stretched several times a day to give her at least a little mobility. She'd scream in response to a stretch of her heel cord. My heart would race then stop with every shriek that pierced the air. Tara's physical senses were so diminished that for her to scream, the pain had to be searing. And then I'd have to turn around and stretch that tight little heel all over again, right through the screeches of agony. After immersing myself in her life through those years of pain and joy (yes, there was joy, too), I finally had to give her up to claim my own life. It was another loss, a second death.

What made the decision even harder was Tara's emotional suffering during the transition. While everything physical and mental was off kilter for Tara, her emotional responses were tuned in just fine. Taking Tara away from Mom and big brother Jaime shattered her world. Jaime was the first person to make her laugh. She idolized him. Everything familiar to her would be gone. In spite of Tara's love for Jaime and me, and our love for her, we had to let her go. There were parts of Jaime's life and my life that had to move on. While we went through this second death together, we had the luxury of planning it.

There was only one home I would consider for Tara — Marge Stratton's. Marge was a grandmotherly RN who ran a residential care home for six disabled children. I met her at group sessions for the kids and was impressed with her affection and sincere interest in her children. And she had experience administering complicated drug therapies. Tara's seizures were grand mal and devastating, requiring heavy drugs and a lot of monitoring. Marge's was the only home for Tara. It was meant to be — miraculously, state funding and Marge's home opened up for Tara at the same time.

What a huge relief. But the weaning process was just beginning for all of us. Tara started at Marge's weekends-only for the first several weeks, then three days a week while I prepared to look for a job. We graduated to four days apart before going to five. The process took six months. By then I had landed a management training position with Wells Fargo Bank. Once I started working, Tara was with me only on weekends.

Now, this sounds much easier than it was. For Tara, every tiny motion was a major triumph of mind over the feeble message system to her muscles. Her hand would struggle to grab me as I laid her in her crib at Marge's. Every muscle in her face pleaded with me to take her with me. These were the only times I remember her crying real tears. My tears stayed inside.

These memories flooded my mind as I spoke with Marge on the morning of Tara's third death — her physical death. Flashbacks and a cacophony of feelings, tuned down by numbness. The guilt flared up first, for leaving Tara all those years with Marge. A rush of pride and joy remembering Tara's ecstasy when given the freedom to smear whipped cream all over her high chair and her clothes, squishing it sensually in her fingers. The poignant sight of her huge brown eyes magnified through bottle-thick glasses. The horrific sense of loss as I snapped to the present and my conversation with Marge.

As Marge and I finished talking, my next thought was of my health. Lupus is stress-induced and this was stress to the max. I was already so sick I could hardly move or stay awake. The doctor would be on my list of calls. But first I'd call Anthony, the love in my life and my partner. If he could leave his office to join me, I could deal with the rest.

Next was Tara's father, my ex-husband, whose voice I did not want to hear. But I felt a sense of compassion for this man who hadn't opened up to let Tara in. I called the school where he taught. He took the call in the administration office, so the conversation was not private for him. I kept asking if he was OK, and he kept saying yes, he was fine. He said he would go back to the classroom to finish the day. We agreed on a mortician and arranged to meet after school to tell Jaime about his sister. A rush of old feelings surfaced as I hung up the phone. I hated it when he pretended everything was all right when it wasn't. That was so typical!

Now, on to the phone call to my mom. Her first concern was for my health. Once a mom always a mom. Even in my grief, this irritated me. I didn't want to be babied. At the same time I felt a tremendous relief that she was lifting some of my burdens. Mom arranged for my sister Laura to drive me to the mortuary.

It was a fast, quiet 75-mile drive to the mortuary. I desperately wanted to see Tara in her natural state, before embalmers got hold of her. I was exhausted beyond anything I'd ever experienced — drained, empty, a floppy rag doll draped across the car seat. I didn't trust my body to carry me through the next phases of Tara's death.

Our rush paid off. I got to Tara's side in time. She lay on her back, pale and still, looking just like she had so much of her life. She wore a pajama top her Grandma Brandy had given her. It was yellow, my favorite color for Tara. The front was adorned with a cherubic angel fast asleep. The lettering read "Our Little Angel." She was. All my love and affection for her rushed up inside me and burst out in a huge shameless wail. I indulged myself, sobbing as long as it took, huddled over her little body.

This time alone with Tara, our little angel, gave me the opportunity to reflect. She was the gentlest person I'd ever met. There was a quiet wisdom about her that made me think she was an old soul. Her physical movements were limited, so she used them sparingly and well. Sometimes she would chuckle to herself as she watched the world rushing around her. And she controlled the world to her liking. She was a brilliant little flirt, getting everyone to stop and fuss over her, as she flashed her dimples to encourage more. Batting her big browns yielded the same manic entertainment. Her eyelashes brushed against her glasses they were so long. She worked her audience into giggles and coos.

Tara could wrap me around her finger with little fake coughs. She'd muster up a tiny "hack," then peer out of the corner of her eye, grinning and waiting for me to stop my busyness to fuss over her and show mock concern. My act was dramatic enough to earn a chuckle from Tara, and another tiny cough to keep the game going. She was all about getting people to slow down, especially me. She accomplished this with minimal motion, to maximum effect ... a little Zen Guru.

Tara was fun! There wasn't much fun in my life at that time. While her complications were burdensome, what stands out are the times she got me to pause. She loved bluesy rock 'n' roll. The louder and heavier the base-tone the better for her diminished senses. We loved old "Cream" albums with Eric Clapton. I'd stop my practical ways and shake her hands to "I Feel Free," snap my fingers, and watch her scrunch her hands, trying to snap in time to the beat. Her face would twist with the effort, sporting a giant grin the whole time. She could hardly contain her ecstasy. Neither could I.

She was my Guru. What did I learn from someone whose life and thoughts were so simple? Just about everything that makes me who I am today. In her short life, she taught me about balance and priorities. I was way off kilter, focusing on minutia and perfection, and pleasing everyone else to my own detriment. Over the years, I learned to juggle important priorities, while keeping Tara's many balls in the air. And I learned the meaning of unconditional love, while being force-fed life's difficult lessons. It was the hard lessons that brought out many of the qualities I like best about myself now.

When Tara was alive, I had to be so practical that there wasn't time or space for feelings. I was meeting her needs, her brother's needs, my educational needs, the household needs, the needs of my marriage (soon to be former marriage), and advocacy needs as federal, state and local funding sources for disabled people were being severely slashed. Sure, I came away with the organizational skills of a CEO. At the same time, I stayed numb most of the years of Tara's life.

Numbness allowed me to function. It was obvious in 1979, as I phased out of my marriage and settled Tara at Marge's, that practicality was overwhelming all other aspects of my life. Any fragments of psychological or spiritual health that remained in my tattered soul were threadbare. The effect of this was wearing down my physical body. I was unaware of it at the time, but I was developing lupus: a chronic disease of the immune system.

-2-

LUPUS

Use minimal motion for maximum effect to survive —

By the time Tara passed away in 1984, I was very ill and on a potent cocktail mix of steroids, anti-inflammatories, and anti-malarials just to keep going each day. Even in my weakened state, I knew that I would never get better until I addressed the emotional issues surrounding life with Tara. I had no idea at the time how difficult that journey would be. Soul searching is hard, hard work.

The lessons I learned and the tactics I used may help you, if you are facing serious personal challenges — whether they relate to your health, family, spirit or career. For me it was a process that required enormous patience as I waded through setbacks and reset my course each time. If you can grasp onto anything from my personal story to feed your own endurance, I encourage you to do so.

As I faced the loss of Tara and the loss of my health, creativity got me through the next chapters of my life. I became like Tara, minimal motion for maximum effect. From that Zen-like state a newfound trust emerged that everything would come out fine — somehow. By leveraging the assets of creativity and trust I gained a fuller life than when I ran on organization and practicality alone.

The transformation did not happen overnight, by any means. It went on for more than 10 years, as I dug out of the health hole I had created: lupus. The hole was so deep I didn't know where to begin. I could not give Tara up, and her spirit overwhelmed me. Her ghost was in my work life, my home life, and my social life. I feared that if I let go of Tara, it would be discounting her entire existence, as if her short life had not mattered. It was so instinctive to hold on that no rationale could loosen my grip.

It would have been impossible to deal with the entire picture at once. Any serious, complex issue is best broken down into smaller, more manageable pieces. My physical health was almost gone, my spiritual health was all tied up in Tara, and I didn't have a clue how to deal with my emotional health since I was numb much of the time. The one straw I could grasp was my mental faculty. I could be creative. I could create a plan.

My plan for recovery started with physical issues. My strength was so low I was sleeping about 22 hours a day. But I refused to let my muscles deteriorate. During 20 minutes of my functional time each day, I exercised to ESPN aerobics shows. I pre-taped them, so I could seize the moment when I had the energy. While the cast members bounced, I gingerly shuffled in place. When they did weights, I inched my half-pounders up and down to the music. My output increased over time as my body allowed, and I headed straight for bed after each session.

My medical focus with doctors at the University of California was to gradually reduce my medication and see if I could avoid a flare-up of lupus. Most of the time I'd get sick again, so we'd bump the dosage back up. It was a little like an ebbing tide. The dosage would go up, but then down a little more than it went up. The next wave up would not be quite so high, and then back down still lower. My ebb and flow of drugs took seven long years to bottom out. I'm thankful that I have been in remission since then.

Even after I became medication-free, exhaustion plagued me. And my immune system was like a baby's. I had been secluded for so long that, as I emerged into the world, I caught every bug that was going around. For several years I was sick with a cold or flu the equivalent of nine months out of 12. My doctors shrugged their shoulders — their drugs couldn't help me with these problems. So I turned to alternative medicine.

I heard about Larry Johnson, a pioneer in magnetic acupuncture. It was a new concept and Larry literally wrote the book on it. I'd try almost anything that made sense, so I made an appointment right away.

Magnetic acupuncture is like traditional acupuncture, using magnets instead of needles. I liked magnets better, because I could tape them on my hands and continue to move around. Larry determined the best magnet pattern and herbal remedy for each of my symptoms and illnesses. He drew hand charts for me, and gave me a set of little magnetic dots to take home and tape on my hands, per his diagrams. Believe it or not, it worked. Beautifully.

I developed a small library of magnet hand patterns that Larry created for various problems. Over time they brought me to a new level of energy and health. I had patterns for aches and pains, increasing energy, reducing fever, and re-balancing the immune system. I wore magnets everywhere I went. People got used to seeing little dots on my hands. They probably thought I was a little dotty in the head too, but it worked, so I didn't care.

During this phase, my energy may have been low but my mind was active. I was on disability leave, and lying in bed so much allowed me the space to use my mind: I came up with a real estate partnership idea that included Anthony (whether he liked it or not). I think he liked it because he drove with me every Sunday to see the open houses for sale. The idea was to get a house in San Francisco with an in-law apartment. We wanted a fixer-upper to profit from the upside of the cosmetic work, as well as rental income. Within six months we owned the dream fixer-upper we had envisioned.

That business project and the physical fitness challenges kept me going. But it was not enough. Crucial to my recovery was the psychological and spiritual work that remained to be done. Tara's spirit still dominated my life. I needed to get perspective on the guilt, love, loss and sadness.

With only a few waking hours available to me each week I invested some of that time on the psychologist's couch and some of that time in more ethereal alternatives. While I am no expert, I attribute my recovery as much to that internal work as to the traditional medicine and physical fitness.

I worked with Linda Brown, a counselor and hypnotherapist. Sometimes I sat on the couch, talking in a traditional psychology format. Other times I'd lie on the couch in a hypnotic trance. Hypnosis got to the core of an issue more quickly — going straight for the subconscious. Years of hostility simmered in my system and, like a cancer, had invaded my body creating "dis-ease" in the form of lupus.

With Linda I concocted a meditative icon that, in my visions, destroyed the demons that caused my deep-seated anger. This creature was a dry, old crone — strong, intense and full of impact. Picture the Wicked Witch in *The Wizard of Oz* and you have the general idea. She was vicious, but oddly enough, she was my protector. As a demon appeared, she blasted it with fire like a dragon, and kept blasting through screams and terror, until the demon was destroyed. If the demon resurfaced through the smoke, she slashed back and forth with a huge sickle until it was reduced to a pile of blood and guts, demolished.

Some of my demons were real people who had inflicted pain on me, often unwittingly. Regardless of their motivations, I harbored that pain as anger. It was hard to get used to blasting them so they'd burn down to ash. The scenes were bloody, violent, and full of roaring flames and desperate howls — more like a grade B horror flick than a soothing meditation. But over time the process worked. Demons stopped coming. Anger simmered down. Depression faded. I began making constructive choices instead of letting life's disasters choose my direction for me.

As I healed from within, I exercised with more vigor, working up to bike rides and weight workouts by being consistent in spite of all the setbacks of lupus. During each setback I continued with mild yoga to keep my muscles going — just get back on and ride after every illness.

The driving force of my recovery was a concentrated blend of traditional and alternative medicines. I couldn't have dealt with so many issues in only one dimension. There were many years of medication for lupus, hypnotherapy, meditation, acupuncture, psychotherapy, diet experimentation, and anything else that made sense. I kept what worked and discarded the rest. The support network I found in all of this kept me going when it looked like there was no end in sight. At times, depression hung so heavy that as I shuffled across the street in a daze, I hoped a car would hit me. "Just get it over with."

But I didn't want to medicate away the pain. I wanted it there so I would know what to deal with. I wanted to get at the pain from the core. Like an onion, every time I'd peel a layer, there was another eye-stinging layer to go. A lot of crying. A lot of patience. I never knew it would be so hard.

What eventually surfaced through all the hardship was a solid spiritual core within me that can never be taken away. This core is wrapped securely in the lessons that emerged through trial and error:

- Use minimal motion for maximum effect.
- Break down complex issues into manageable bites.

- Do what you can — even a tiny step will get you started.
- If that step doesn't work, look for alternatives that *will* work.
- If those alternatives don't work, don't be afraid to seek help.
- Lessons must embrace the whole person — physical, mental, emotional and spiritual.

These lessons can help with the catastrophic issues we all eventually face in life. They can also be applied to achieving goals in our business and personal lives, as you'll see in later chapters when we put together a work-travel life. I hope you can use what I learned the hard way to overcome and avoid trials and errors in your own life.

-3-

FLASHBACKS

Recall childhood memories to boost confidence and identify talents —

We all have times in our lives that we can look back on with pride: when we were at our best, using our strongest traits to overcome challenges. Each person's stories are different, but the lesson remains the same — you can recall earlier memories to boost your confidence and see where your talents lie. In my case, I had sunk so low that first I had to assess the damage — so I would know what to rebuild.

The most difficult phase of the healing process was when I spent more time *in* bed than out. My attempts to be productive were feeble at best. There was no definitive prognosis with lupus, so it was hard to set goals for myself. I was completely and utterly lost without goals. I had driven myself to achieve since I was a little kid. My identity was all wrapped up in my successes. I knew nothing else.

Even as I started to get better, my old confidence had completely eroded away. I realized how timid I was when I went to my first social gathering without Anthony. Before I lost my health, I relished the idea of meeting new people. But now I felt like a different person than when I worked at the bank. What would I talk about? I wasn't doing anything. At the party I tried to keep quiet, but people kept coming up and asking me, "What do you do for a living?" to start a conversation. I was at a loss for words.

I didn't want to be a downer and talk about illness and

death at a party. But illness and death were my life. I was too tired to drum up the curiosity to ask people about themselves, which would have deflected attention from me. I side-stepped their questions, answering that I was on a leave of absence from my banking career, to reflect on my priorities. Actually that was pretty good! But I was rattled by the experience. There was no inner drive left to rev up my old determination. Maybe I didn't want to have that kind of determination again. But how would I function?

During my hours in bed, I pondered those issues. On one level my life-long focus to succeed had driven me into the ground, but on another, it could be my saving grace. I had memories I could tap, from when I was striving, energetic and competent. If I dredged up clear images of my once-enthusiastic self, I could imitate my former self. If muscle memory kicked in, I'd regain some of those dormant, positive feelings.

When did all this ambition take hold in me? Reflecting back, my desire to please others started when I was five years old. At the dinner table every night, Dad would grill my big brother Donnie in an attempt to maximize Donnie's intellectual powers. "How do you spell 'encyclopedia'?"

"Uh, e-n-c, uh, ency, uh — i?"

"No! Y!" I chimed in. Donnie didn't appreciate the help, but it got Dad's attention. By the time I reached the ripe old age of six, I was spelling "encyclopedia" at dinner with no visual aids, reciting the capitals of the United States, and whatever else pleased my father. Dad pressed both of us on to more difficult questions with a sharp rebuke if we were too slow or, heaven forbid, if we guessed wrong.

Dinner became a high anxiety grilling every night. Mom finally started making a separate dinner for Dad, so we'd get a break from being quiz-kids. The tradition of two seatings for dinner continued for the rest of our lives at my parents' house. But the seed of ambition was already firmly planted in me.

My political career began a few short years later in the third grade when Ann Taylor nominated me for room representative. Elections were held the first month of school. I didn't even know that Ann knew who I was yet. Being nominated was a compliment. To make it even better, I won the election. I had no idea my fellow classmates regarded me so highly, and I was in awe. The grownups in my family were proud and my desire to please others by being ambitious was reinforced.

In fourth, fifth and sixth grades, I was elected not only to room representative but also class treasurer, secretary, vice president, and president. I won student body presidency in the sixth grade only after going outside, the evening before the election, to wish on a star *and* pray (covering all bases). In my prayer I said if I got to be president, I'd never ask for anything else again, ever. I doubt it made any difference, but I won.

So there I was, a little sixth grader, meeting with the school principal monthly to set the agenda for the next student body meeting. Each month I stood on a stage behind a podium with a microphone, speaking to an audience of about 200 children and parents: moving through the agenda, introducing speakers and participating in forums. I thought this was normal.

As I lay in bed recovering, and thought about my childhood successes, I saw that they did not necessarily come easily. But I had not been deterred. In all of my school years, if I failed at anything, I got right back up knowing I could do it better next time. I didn't flinch. When public failure was a risk, I assessed how badly I wanted to make it to the other end before charging in. And then, look out!

Near the end of eighth grade, elections came up for ninth grade student body officers and cheerleaders. I wanted to be a cheerleader but didn't think I had a chance. Cheerleaders were selected by a popularity contest, not athletic ability. One day during the sign-up period, I was walking from gym class with Nancy, who was a year older and a cheerleader. She asked if I would run. I gave all the usual excuses.

"Cindy and Terry and all the other popular girls will win, so what's the point? It would be embarrassing to lose." Nancy has no idea how she influenced my life when she responded, "I thought the same thing last year and wasn't going to run. My brother said, 'If you really want it, you won't let those excuses get in the way. If you don't try, you'll never know if you could have won.' Do you really want it?"

I knew at that moment that I did want it. I wanted it enough to risk the embarrassment of losing. I wanted it enough to figure out what I needed to do to become a cheerleader. I signed up to run. That night, I turned once again to the stars and my prayers. I said, with complete sincerity and great passion, that if I could get *this* I wouldn't ask for anything else, ever again.

My brother Donnie created really cool posters for my campaign. Friends helped me come up with a strong routine for the tryouts. My mother worked hard, sewing a little pink skirt with suspenders for the day before the election when I performed in front of 600 students. I sweated it until the last moment. It was a close call, I knew.

On election day, the principal announced the winners over the intercom. I stopped breathing I was so tense. I held my breath through the list of officers, class representatives, and the first three cheerleaders. The names were alphabetical, and I was second-to-last. I won! I must have been blue in the face by then, but a whoop of relief burst out and I finally got air. Friends jumped all over me and whooshed me out the classroom door. The first ninth grader I saw was Nancy. I actually got to thank her. If she hadn't talked to me, I wouldn't have taken the risk.

As adults we often forget how wise children can be. We also don't realize how powerful our own childhood memories are. These memories, which we've possessed all along and may have almost forgotten, are precious resources to draw upon for guidance during life changes or crises.

Part of my confidence as a kid came from being able to laugh at my embarrassing moments. It gave me the freedom to risk failure. A rather silly event marked the first time I clearly saw the value of laughing at myself. I was in a great mood one day as I entered art class. I bounced and twirled my way to my seat. I think the floors had just been waxed because I slipped in a giant spiral motion right down onto my keister, legs spinning above me. Instead of jumping up as if nothing happened and turning red in the face, a spark of genius popped into my head: Hold that position, legs in the air for dramatic effect, and laugh. Everyone joined in, laughing with me rather than at me. My confidence was stronger after that as I saw that mistakes are OK and can even be maximized to great effect. Just face them head on.

As a cheerleader I had all kinds of opportunities to overcome teenage embarrassment. Once, when I was to teach the student body a new school song, performing solo and a cappella, I developed laryngitis. At the rally, I had just enough voice to whisper and maybe muster a hoarse word or two. Rather than get someone else to do the song, I made it a comedy routine. I squeaked and croaked the melody into the microphone, then encouraged everyone to sing along. Of course, they were laughing as loud as they were singing. But it was a memorable moment, got a write-up in the school paper, and everyone learned the song really fast because I got their attention with my froggy voice.

As I reflected on my life, I found that the younger I was in my memories of success or wisdom, the more positive the effect on my rehabilitation. I knew if I could be inventive and self-assured at an early age, I could do it as a grownup. No excuses.

So, I went back to even earlier times in my memories, and I found another source of strength. For a long time, from about three to nine years old, my fantasy world reigned supreme. I was free and strong in this world. When grownups were overbearing, I retreated to my fantasies for comfort. The key figure in this world was a great white Pegasus, like the one on the Flying A gas station sign. He was magnificent: a winged horse I could ride whenever I wanted, wherever I wanted. We'd fly over the tops of the neighborhood houses and into my imaginary worlds. The freedom and the power were intoxicating. The experience was so real I could feel the horse's body heat and the wind on my face as we flew. It was an escape that exhilarated me no matter what else was going on in my world. I felt all-powerful.

Pegasus was my protector, much like the old crone in my adult meditations. But Pegasus was a regal vision, unlike the ugly, shriveled crone. Pegasus was white (in contrast to the dark, ominous crone) and young (the crone was ancient). The heroic Pegasus in my childhood fantasies infused me with confidence.

As an adult, was I living what I had valued as the little girl who loved Pegasus? Was I free and in my own power? Hardly. But flashbacks to those dreams of Pegasus reminded me what I valued in my core. I decided, as I lay in bed, that every activity I added to my life would be true to my core beliefs in freedom and personal power.

I don't want to rule out adult memories as a tool for growing and healing. It is wise to recall any positive period and use it as a guide out of a quagmire. I also gained strength from looking back at my busy, productive time as a young mother.

When Jaime was little, I could go, and go, and go: as a mom, college student, cook, seamstress, calligrapher, and top-notch craftsperson. I handcrafted every cookie that went into a lunch box. My soups, breads and pies were to die for. Jaime wore coveralls made by his mom. Every Christmas gift to family members was crocheted, starting in July. Not to mention the hand-calligraphed menus I was paid to print for local restaurants, and the handwritten music sheets musicians used to copyright their masterpieces. Those were for "pin money" I used to say. All that, plus straight A's in college. (We won't count my lowly "B" in badminton, which "destroyed" my grade-point average). And, I was assistant to the head of the home economics department.

All of that frenzied activity was a bit much. But I learned a lot from looking back at that era. Upon closer examination, I could either tap into that drive or find a new source of strength and conviction.

The motive behind all that domesticity was hardly domestic bliss. My efforts were driven by a desire to be the best mother I could for Jaime, and securing our financial future through academic excellence. My activities were scheduled so that I could be with Jaime full time, except while in class. Then he was with his dad or his Grandma Brandy. The domestic projects were also driven by my need to stretch our whopping $235 a month income (my husband and I were starving students). It was the most prolific time in my life.

Flashes to the past can also teach us where we went wrong, so we don't repeat our mistakes. You may see already that I was a controlling young adult. It only got worse as I got a little older. During my recovery from lupus, I relied on memories of my fanaticism to keep myself toned down.

When I was living that busy life as a young mother, I wasn't content with my current accomplishments. So my next creation was going to be a big one. It was springtime. I had been on birth control pills for several years. But now, I wanted to create another baby. If I was to have another child, I felt this was the perfect time — not because it was perfect for my marriage, which was faltering badly by then: We were both so absorbed in our own busyness that there was no space left for the relationship. And my biological clock was certainly not ticking. I was all of 23 years old when this scheme came into being. But it was the perfect time for a baby because it fit so neatly into my grand schedule.

The grand schedule consisted of finishing all the nutrition and Spanish language coursework that could be done locally. When the baby was two years old, I could commute to San Francisco State University and complete my last year of a degree in nutrition with a minor in Spanish. By the time our second child was in first grade, I would have my graduate degree and could teach at the college level. Perfect. The baby would have to be born during semester break of the following year so that I wouldn't miss a semester of school, heaven forbid. The whole plan would be ruined if the baby was born mid-semester and I missed any school.

The plan was executed impeccably: off the pill in February, two months for the ovaries to kick into gear, and pregnant by May. Done deal. The baby would be born late January of the next year, 1976. No time for morning sickness or tired afternoons — just keep on truckin'.

By that time, Jaime's dad had his teaching credential and was teaching school. Perfect again. We had a real job in the family and could even buy a clothes washer and dryer, a giant freezer, a new vacuum, a super-duper Kitchen Aid mixer, and a new Volkswagen bus for our expanding family. I was in major nesting mode.

January came along and I had completed a heavy load of classes, plus a childbirth course. For spring semester I scheduled only a conversational Spanish class, while I recovered from childbirth. I'd resume 10 or so units in the fall. Everything was humming along beautifully.

One evening as semester break started, I cooked a full turkey dinner with all the trimmings, just for John, Jaime and me. There were stacks of containers on the counter in which to store leftovers for easy meals after the baby was born. We were relaxing at the kitchen table in over-stuffed bliss when, "Ooh," the first little contraction. Then, "Ow!" Another one. Oh no! I still had to finish sewing my robe for the hospital. The kitchen was a mess. Baby announcements had to be addressed. This was happening too soon!

I shifted into high gear and left the job of timing contractions to John. I sliced turkey, divided it into containers, and added stuffing, potatoes and gravy to each one before sealing it. Then, out came the quilted fabric I had cut in the shape of a robe and belt. I sat, informing John of each contraction, while I tacked the spots where darts would be stitched into the robe. It was no use; there was too much detailing in the robe to finish it. The sewing ground to a halt. But! I could address envelopes. So I wrote the rest of the evening away. Now it was time to pack the car and take Jaime to Grandma Brandy's house where we waited for the high sign from the doctor to go to the hospital.

We finally got the go-ahead to proceed to the maternity ward and little Tara Grace was born early that morning. My dream had come true: I had a boy and a girl now. I wore my old robe and it worked just fine. And there were still eight days to recover before I had to return to class. I didn't miss a beat.

What was driving me to be so frenzied? I had a compelling

need to do right by my children and still have my own achievements. Every scholastic and career goal I set for myself still allowed me to be "Mom." I had a picture in my head of a good mother: It included being with the children as much as possible, and yet taking steps to have my own identity and accomplishments. That meant living life at double speed around the clock. Motherhood was magical for the strength it brought me. Life was all about responsibility for two tiny, helpless individuals who needed me.

In later years as I recovered from lupus and rebuilt my life, I needed a new source for motivation. Jaime was a fairly independent teenager, and Tara was a spirit in my world, not a responsibility. The drive had to come from within me, for myself and nobody else. And it just wasn't coming. How happy was I anyway, when I buzzed through life like a worker bee on speed? Maybe I needed to re-evaluate: perhaps combine the best of my past with what I was learning through my illness in the present.

-4-

HEALING
While building, be true to core values —

The ambition I cultivated from childhood increased each year as I grew older. I loved the spotlight. And I loved a challenge, especially if I came out on top. This would have been fine if ambition didn't compound like the interest on a loan. By the time I was 32 years old, I was so focused on my career at Wells Fargo Bank, and on climbing the corporate ladder, that I had become a steamroller. No one could get in my way, or I rolled over the top of them with blasts of enthusiasm for my opinions. My supercharged energy grew so out of proportion that it became toxic: another likely cause of the lupus.

Just one year later, at the ripe old age of 33, I was humbled big time. I was so sick from lupus and the loss of Tara that I was on long-term disability. There was no career left to use as a social crutch. So who was I? I wrestled with that issue. As I healed, I didn't want to just find my old identity. That had been unsatisfying. Based on what I knew about lupus, it was best to downsize my ambitions and emphasize moderation instead.

Easier said than done. As I experienced phases of feeling better, ambitious dreams crept in and dominated my thoughts. If I acted on those thoughts, I'd get knocked down into bed to do penance, sick once again. It felt like being zapped with a stun gun; I'd get so sick, so fast. My body wouldn't let me get away with it anymore. I knew deep inside that I'd never get better physically or emotionally until I could stand on my own, with humility and calm, without relying on illness to tone me down.

It was hard to balance my striving nature with a moderation I had never known but needed to develop. The idea of attempting anything and not getting completely carried away with it was so foreign. There was no inner thermostat in me that said "too hot" or "too cold." I knew no limits. I lived by the credo that if I wanted it enough, I could do what it took to accomplish it. And I literally ran myself into the ground doing just that.

My new credo had to be completely different. "Ground zero" was my motto. It meant that I did nothing that was to please others or was an obligation — nothing, zero, zilch. I reached ground zero during my phase of sleeping 22 hours a day, which lasted several months. I spent time eating and on cleanliness, 20 minutes of exercises daily and saw several doctors weekly. That was it.

Then came the hard part, adding back into my life only what I wanted to do. This was very foreign to me. I didn't allow myself to do anything "constructive." If I wanted to walk, I walked. If it was a daily commitment in my mind, an "obligation," I didn't walk. Simplicity can be so difficult for a naturally ambitious person like me.

Over the next year or so, as I started to feel a little better, there was more awake-time — maybe eight hours on a good day. I had more time with well-chosen friends. I couldn't have a wide group of friends because it was too tiring. There was time to read books about healing. I traveled overseas with Anthony. He made the arrangements, hoisted my luggage into the overhead bins, and was patient about my many naps. I got to relax and enjoy all the good stuff. Now, this probably sounds like a cushy job: relax, enjoy, and be pampered. But for me, letting someone else do everything for me was unnatural. I felt guilty. I felt out of control. I felt useless. But it was needed in order to get better.

My self-image and how I presented myself transformed during this time. Instead of being about my work, I discussed everything except work. I was about travel, cooking, decorative projects, what I read, what I was learning, and being a friend. I became more interested in other people's stories. What made them who they are?

I knew my body could not support me in a demanding career. How would I survive financially? After I reached ground zero and was rebuilding my life, every activity I added would be true to my core beliefs in freedom and personal power. Even work.

I had economic issues to face as I was being true to this freedom and personal power. After a year, my short-term disability was up. It was time to apply for long-term Social Security Disability Income (SDI) which is easier said than done. Though I could not sit up for more than an hour at a time and my blood tests showed raging lupus, the Social Security Administration was not satisfied. They explained that I would have to demonstrate inability to perform any work of any kind for even a short time each day. My inability to work at what I was trained to do was not sufficient to qualify for SDI.

My doctors would have done anything in their power to get this income for me. They wrote letters and referred me to attorneys specializing in this area of law. All of the qualifying questions had to be answered, "I can't." "I can't stand for more than so many minutes, I can't lift this weight, I can't do that." The more "I can'ts" I could come up with, the better my chances of getting SDI. My appearance was a hindrance: I had clear skin and was thin (medications killed my appetite). I looked like the current trend in skinny fashion models as I walked into each office. Doctors felt I'd ultimately qualify for SDI, but because I looked healthy, I would spend a year or so with attorneys to win.

Would it really be a win? I didn't take long to decide: I'd rather do without the income. By saying "I can't" for an entire year, I would limit my mind and my recovery. If I was successful and got SDI, then I'd be afraid to get better for fear of losing the money.

This was a scary decision. With no clear prognosis for lupus, my doctors could not assure me that I'd ever get better than I was at that time. As my health improved over the years, there were lean times when I'd have loved the extra income, but I'm glad I didn't pursue it. My life would still be diminished if I had chosen the disability path.

While the SDI issue brewed in my mind, life began to take a little bit of shape again. My vision of being a landlord came to pass as Anthony and I worked on our fixer-upper house and apartment. I pulled weeds, planted gardens, painted the interior, and practiced landlording on Eleanor, the easygoing tenant downstairs. I kept the books and learned about such goodies as depreciation for tax purposes. I spent a couple of hours a day being a "mini-mogalette," planning the renovation and resale of this house so we could graduate to a four-unit apartment building. There was finally a venue for my ambitions, within the scope of my physical limitations. Still, sleeping 16 hours a day meant keeping goals simple and focused.

The small disability check I got from Wells Fargo each month wasn't enough to make ends meet. As the house renovations neared completion, I had to figure out a source of part-time income. My friends BJ and Terry, the real estate brokers who got us into our new venture, encouraged me to get my license and join their office. They'd work around my heavy sleep requirements.

My foremost thought was to solve my immediate problem: creating income in a way that I could physically handle. BJ and Terry's generous offer could alleviate that concern. In my panic about financial survival, I didn't think about whether real estate sales fit my core values. So I gathered my limited energy and initiated the steps to become a Realtor.

I got off to a shaky start in real estate school. It may seem like I had plenty of energy, given the work I had done on the house. But that was accomplished tiny bits at a time, with the brunt of the physical work performed by Anthony. I'd work half an hour, then go to bed until I could rally again. Now, with real estate school, I had to ride a bus to class (still too weak to drive), sit, and take notes for three hours before riding back home.

Lessons from Tara came back to me. Minimal motion gets maximum results. Keep it simple. My little Guru. I blended naptime with study time, and shifted smoothly between the two. Naps were now on the sofa instead of the bed. I'd doze off, dreaming sweet dreams, with my books in my lap. As soon as I was awake enough to concentrate, I remained in position, reached for my pencil, and started studying, not even lifting my head.

It worked. I whizzed through real estate school in a couple of months, flat on my back most of the time. The state exam was a breeze. Now it was time for the next big test: my first day in BJ and Terry's office. I had been home, sick and secluded, for most of the previous four years, deprived of the usual business interactions.

The others in BJ's office knew what they were doing and had tons of energy to accomplish their tasks. Meanwhile I had a paralyzing combination of shyness and lack of faith that my body could get up to speed. I was scared to death, shaky, and my head was ringing. Luckily the office had an open floor plan. I watched and listened, and figured out what to do bit by bit. I had office time in the morning, then walked up the street to my house and slept the rest of the day.

The late '80s were a boom real estate period in San Francisco. After my second sale, I finally let go of my security blanket, the small-but-helpful monthly disability check from Wells Fargo. I was able to work part-time and still win "rookie of the year" for the office my first year. I was officially launched. Minimal motion was getting maximum results. Simplicity. Thank you, Tara.

Real estate sales alleviated my immediate financial worries. However, as I continued to work in the industry, dissatisfaction bubbled to the surface. Real estate didn't fit my goal of completely healing. My craving for monetary sustenance caused me to ignore one of my biggest lessons — take care of the whole person, including physical, emotional and spiritual aspects.

I would sit amid the frenzied hustle at BJ's office and all I could think of was nap time. Phones rang off the hook, agents gabbed into headsets, and people bustled in and out, files tucked under their arms. I couldn't stand the chaos and constant interruption in the office. It drove me nuts!

I was also afraid because I couldn't put in enough hours to get the job done. Even with only three clients I couldn't keep up. Lauralee wanted to buy way out on the edge of the city where prices were low. Tomoko wanted to buy in the heart of Noe Valley. And Megan wanted the Pacific Heights area. I was spinning in circles as I raced from one end of San Francisco to the other. There was not enough time left to drum up new business, learn how to put deals together, and attend the necessary meetings. It couldn't be done in only four hours a day, and I needed my nap!

I also resented all the calls to my home when I was trying to sleep. Clients managed to find a real estate sign on the "perfect" house when I was trying to sleep! There was no peace anymore.

The office was a madhouse and my home was no longer my castle.

I was aggravated by inner conflict, and wondered, "What is there to drive me?" Part of me wanted to slow down and take care of myself. Part of me resented the need to stop and take care of myself. I needed to re-evaluate. But boy, old habits and attitudes are deeply rooted. Every time I felt better I wanted to charge in again. I wanted to do it all. And I really wanted to take a nap, too.

Those issues whirled around in my head for years. I had to leave them unresolved while I concentrated on supporting myself. I ultimately progressed well in real estate. At the same time, I suffered a sad deconstruction in my personal life. Anthony and I went our separate ways. We had shared wonderful experiences and supported each other through some of life's tragedies: the death of his father to cancer, my lupus, Tara's death. We meant a lot to each other, but it was time to move on. We sold our four-unit building. Yes, we had graduated to a four-unit building according to the original plan. We separated our possessions and our hearts and went in new directions.

I shifted into "mini-mogulette" mode after the breakup and bought a large apartment building with a partner. The stress of my expanding real estate business, and the heart-breaking separation from Anthony, took a toll on my health. But now I had tools to work with. There were a network of doctors, my trusty magnets, a masseuse, two chiropractors, a yoga teacher, and a host of others. I was frustrated at the frequent setbacks, the expense in time and money for health services, and the need to sleep so much. But I was seeing progress. Sure, there were days when I wondered if the problems would ever end: Those days were now fewer and farther between.

As good days started to outnumber the bad, I set new goals for myself. I felt that I would get a steadier lifestyle in many ways if I went into real estate sales management. So, with misgivings, I left BJ's office and went to a larger company, Pacific Union. It was more corporate and would give me the needed experience to go into management. And it expanded my life in many ways.

I started making new friends. In the course of that, none of the new friends knew me as a person who was always sick and weak. No one knew me as the woman whose daughter died — unless I felt close enough to tell them. It gave me a chance to try on a new persona, that of a healthy person. It was another phase in letting go of old illness and tragedy.

All of this took place about eight years after Tara's death and I was finally facing the spiritual aspects of the healing process. In my work with Linda Brown, she knew that Tara was still a dominating force in every aspect of my life. Linda performed several deep hypnosis sessions with me. In that incredible dream state I was finally released from Tara. It felt like Tara's spirit had to hang around until I was well on my way to learning the lessons she had been teaching. Use minimal motion to maximum effect. Simplicity. Take care of yourself. That's my little Guru.

For me, the hypnotic release was like going through a fourth death with Tara — a spiritual death. She now had no hold on me. I had no hold on her. This time the death was liberating: as if Tara's ghost was free to move on, and I was free to live a full life.

So many years after losing Tara she is still in me every day as I live and breathe. But now there is no obligation. What remains are bittersweet memories that I cherish, and the valuable lessons I learned. The sadness is finally sweet, and welcome. The journey so far has led to an incredible blend of work, travel, new challenges, play and relaxation. I'm finally free to choose a joyous life. Again, thank you, Tara.

As I grew healthier, some of my new values, which fed the

healing process, didn't fit in the corporate world. I learned a lot at Pacific Union, and got tremendous support from management in expanding my sales and marketing acumen. However selling real estate was not fulfilling anymore. I wanted life to be about more than just making money. Not that making money is bad, but making it the focal point of my existence wasn't cutting it for me. I didn't feel like I was performing a valuable service anymore. I was no longer willing to work the long, odd hours to keep that business going.

Don't get me wrong. I admire every successful Realtor I meet. They are a dedicated, hard-working bunch who constantly protect their clients' interests. But almost every one of them who is truly honest will admit that his/her primary motivation is $-$-$.

Of course, each time I got serious about leaving the business, I closed a sizable deal, received a big check, and became re-addicted to the money. Gradually other ventures surfaced, allowing me to work at home part time while also selling real estate. As part-time opportunities became more substantive, I found I liked the lifestyle. It took awhile to make the choice to completely leave real estate. When I did, I never looked back.

The funny thing is that some of my health caregivers knew all along that my quest for the almighty dollar was contributing to my illness. They never came out and said so because they knew I had to figure it out for myself. A couple of years after leaving real estate, I ran into a chiropractor who used a unique healing method. I had worked with her for years. But it had been a long time since I'd seen her. She was curious: "What are you doing these days?"

"I'm finally out of real estate. I started doing these 'home expert' segments for the Channel 4 daytime news. You know, kind of like Martha Stewart."

"Oh-h-h. No wonder I never see you anymore. You're out of

real estate!" She laughed. She knew that getting out of the rat race was one of the main reasons I was well enough not to need her services. I was being creative again — truer to my core values.

Tapping Into *Curiosity*

Elizabeth Scott

***Curiosity** is all about being eager to know. Curiosity breeds desire. Desire begets self-discipline. From discipline is born the action that makes dreams come true. None of it can happen without curiosity. Curiosity drives the bold steps needed to realize a dream. When curiosity is strong enough it transforms into courage. Find your curiosity and the rest will follow. The next chapters pose many questions about the work-travel life. Consider them carefully.*

Rock your status quo.

Elizabeth Scott

-5-

TRIAL AND ERROR

"If at first you don't succeed, try, try again" as the old saying goes. Admire other lifestyles — try them on for size —

As my health returned, my personal finances headed south. Of course this caused internal conflict and resulted in some trials and tribulations during that time. But I found that the path of austerity carried me to a better place in the long run.

I think of it as lessons in simplicity, going from materialism to a sort of idealism. The lessons in simplicity started in my real estate days before my financial troubles. Each time I took a vacation and went adventuring in Europe or Mexico, I delved into whatever community I was visiting. As an incurable people-watcher, I observed the differences in behavior and attitudes outside the United States. I got to know neighbors and relatives of my foreign friends, and compared lifestyles and priorities as I conversed with them.

In Greece, happy couples rode tandem on motorbikes through city streets, satisfied with simple vehicles. Prestige wasn't a concern. Transportation and romance seemed to be what counted. The people I befriended on Greek Islands were well-traveled business people who spent each winter in a different part of the world. But they might not own a car at all. And their apartments were simply furnished.

In England, I enjoyed the home of some business associates. Their refrigerator was as small as those we Americans have in recreational vehicles. Their home was a two-story Victorian with lots of space, but they did not need a large refrigerator or glitzy kitchen. They owned just a few basic outfits or suits for work. Georgina would head off to her job as an editor in a classic black skirt and sweater, with a well-chosen scarf to accent her auburn hair and wearing a comfortable pair of flats. She'd hop onto her bicycle and ride across London to her job. She was attractive, fit, and saw no need for our American obsession with clothing or fancy cars. She'd rather save the money for an exotic train trip through India and Asia. She eventually spent an entire year touring those areas.

In Spain, I observed families spending evenings at Karaoke parties, which were very popular there. Children were treated with the same respect as adults, and they were included in the late-night fun. I noticed that Spanish children and teenagers did not express the hyperactivity or disrespect we seem to take for granted in American kids. They were soft-spoken and polite. The adults were liberated and had a high level of self-acceptance. At the beach, I saw mothers of young children swim topless, unashamed of their bodies, stretchmarks and all. It was common and no one was shocked by it.

In Mexico, I honed my Spanish talking philosophy with my friend Alberto's grandfather. He had lived in the Midwest during the 1920s as a migrant laborer. While in America he and his fellow workers did not mix with Americans or learn English. But he was an observant man. He saw the intensity of Americans and wanted no part of it. He said, "Why should we envy Americans? They are such a sad bunch. They think too much about work and money, and not enough about what is really important. They go to a party and sit on the sidelines, worrying about what others will think. They are inhibited. Look at us Mexicans! We sing with gusto, we love to dance, and we are unafraid of romance. We love our children. As a group we are happy. We do not see Americans with such light spirits. They are too serious and materialistic."

Much of what I saw in other countries I embraced. I wanted to adopt their simpler values, which made it hard to return home. One time, on my way back from three weeks in Europe, I was given an American edition of *ELLE* magazine to read on the plane. As I thumbed through it, I saw photographs and articles whose authors obsessed over the perfect manicure and skin exfoliation treatment, the year's hottest makeup techniques, the latest hairstyles, skinny bodies, the trendiest clothes *plus* the ideal boyfriend and how to keep him (*never* let him see you without makeup, heaven forbid). If I didn't feel bad enough yet, there were the stories about what was hot and not so hot for the season. I started fearing that I'd be a fashion "no," passé before my time. The magazine was a major lesson in how to be insecure and superficial. "Oh-h-h yeah. I forgot about all that stuff. Welcome back to America."

Upon re-entry into American life, I visited Linda Brown for several sessions on her couch to get pumped up again to go out and make money. My real estate sales suffered each time I left the country because I returned with a favorable impression of the pared-down European lifestyle. I resisted the materialism of the real estate world. To kick-start my business again, I'd have to recharge psychologically to go out there and succeed.

Ultimately I concluded that maybe I didn't need to work at a job where I had to artificially pump myself up to perform well. Maybe I could simplify my life and be true to my own ideals. As these thoughts started to dominate my thinking, my choices began to reflect the new me. I moved from a large San Francisco flat to a small one-bedroom apartment, north of the city, on the water in Marin County. The location was calming, and the apartment was *much* less expensive. There was less pressure to work long hours just to keep a roof over my head.

As I pared down, I sold my heavy, dark antique furnishings. They were exchanged for lighter woods, glass and rattan to complement my new sunlit apartment. I got rid of the second set of porcelain china and the second set of sterling flatware. I sold the BMW and got a Honda. I used the money from selling my possessions to purchase a laptop computer, printer and cell phone. I was getting lean and mean, light and agile.

I still enjoy nice things and probably always will. The big change was that I was no longer willing to be a slave to my possessions, or to any "thing." Once I felt a sense of slavery to anything, I let go of the offending item. This new value system left me free to enjoy quality possessions that added to my sense of well-being and to let go of anything that sapped energy from my well-being.

As this paring-down took place, I started to notice changes in my behavior. I used to drive in the fast lane even when there was no reason to hurry. My normally polite persona transformed into a maniacal monster behind the wheel of a car. On any given day you could see me honking, cutting through traffic and flipping people off. My passengers gasped as I caught air racing up and down San Francisco hills. But that was now a part of the old me. Suddenly the new me stopped for pedestrians, drove the speed limit and waited my turn. Without even trying, I was calmer.

But I still hadn't found equilibrium. With all this calm came a collapse in my income. I hadn't yet learned to relax and produce at the same time. I could rela-a-a-x. Or I could run, run, ru-u-n! But I couldn't relax and run at the same time. So my real estate sales bottomed out as I transformed from a type A to a type B or C. As I met with my sales manager to try to rev things up, our sessions became more about her trying to get me motivated again. And it just wasn't happening.

It was a hard choice to leave what was familiar. But it was time to take the risk in order to seek more satisfaction. I dabbled in real estate lending because it allowed me to have sane working hours, and I could work from home several days a week. Starting that kind of business in a down economy was not the best idea, however, and it went nowhere.

While I was floundering in my attempts to make money, I met a neighbor who was an executive recruiter in the optical sales industry. She also worked at home, so we started taking walks together to break up the workday. We'd speed walk and speed talk the whole way. As we shared ideas, we realized we might have a shared business interest. Sharon's recruiting business was more than she could handle, and my lending business was not enough: Maybe I could do some research for her in between making loans. And it worked.

Sharon taught me the ins and outs of finding the right people for the right positions and how to interview candidates over the phone. I could quickly give her the research she needed, and it was an ideal part-time job for me. Over several years of experimentation, as I tried to find my career niche, the executive research always filled a gap.

My real estate lending career died a merciful death so I knew I had to get something else going. Executive research was not enough by itself. I was now willing to get even riskier with my choices. I had pared down my life for a reason: to gain the freedom to take risks. And all new choices were to be consistent with that. It was time to assess my life and start using more of my talents than the standard business world would use.

I was immersed in self-examination. With the help of a friend, and career consultant, Dan Sheridan (and the book he recommended, *What Color Is Your Parachute?* I devised a plan that used some of my dormant talents. Public speaking had always been a favorite part of my jobs in marketing and sales management at Wells Fargo. Also I loved the creative expression of the domestic arts I had used to make ends meet when my children were younger: cooking, sewing, decorating and crafts.

Although I had other talents, I kept coming back to these two: speaking and domestic arts. How could I use these abilities to make a living? The avenue I chose was not an easy one — television. But at least I had a focus. True to my aggressive childhood personality, I charged off in search of my goal. Within two months I was introduced to the news director at the NBC station in San Francisco. We hit it off, and in a few weeks, I was working on camera as Channel 4's "Home Expert."

I was in my element. I loved doing the research, making the props, and taping the shows. It was a grand time meeting television news personalities and taping shows with them. In addition to the TV shows, I was doing radio and television commercials. The work was loads of fun. My parents were proud. I was proud. So what was the problem? It was time-consuming work with only part-time pay. It was not solving my economic problems. And it kept me tied down to the San Francisco area at all times. There was no time to get away, even for weekend trips out of town.

When a news segment or commercial is in production, the producer tends to call at the last minute to get voice or camera talent. If I was unavailable more than once, they stopped calling. No muss, no fuss. So, to stay accessible, I wasn't traveling. And the long hours of preparation for news stories were hard on my health. In addition, I had to keep up the executive search work to stay afloat financially. Gee, my attempts at simplification were not working here.

I didn't want to give up the TV work yet, so I cut expenses further by giving up my apartment. Impetuosity has never been one of my key personality traits, but here I was giving notice on my apartment, with nowhere to go. This was new territory. I trimmed my possessions to the bare minimum. Friends came out of the woodwork offering me a place in their homes. It was gratifying to know that people would come forward, unasked.

I tried a couple of short-term situations and then accepted my friend Al's kind offer to share his house. It was a large, modern home in the hills of Tiburon with beautiful views of Sausalito and the bay. When my sister came over for a barbecue she said, "Gee, Liz, you should write a book — *Homeless and Happy.*" Really, I was homeless. But what a way to go.

However, I couldn't rely on Al's generosity forever. The entire three months I lived there I was looking for the right live-in apartment manager position. I had my real estate broker's license and felt I could combine that part of my business background with the current TV work to complete the income picture.

Once I became an apartment manager, I still had a dilemma. Sure, my costs were down, but my life was even less flexible than before. Not only was I tied to the TV work, I was also tied to the apartments 24 hours a day, seven days a week. People were knocking on my door at 11 at night to complain about noisy neighbors. The fire alarm would go off at four in the morning. Joe, the apartment owner, was very flexible about my need to be away during television tapings. He had bargained for a *live-in* manager, however. So travel was pretty much out. The arrangement started to feel like a giant step backward.

In time I developed a working relationship with my neighbor, Ed, the back-up apartment manager. Ed was happy to cover for me when I went out of town. As a thank-you upon my return,

I'd barbecue him a steak dinner accompanied by his favorite, Chivas Regal. We had a workable system. I continued to work my tail off combining apartment management, TV tapings, and some executive search work. I could also get out and have a travel adventure once in awhile.

One Christmas season, I taped an especially demanding series of news segments on cooking and craft projects for the holidays. I was exhausted and decided to get out of town right after Christmas Eve. My friend Nicki and I drove up to Sun Valley, Idaho, on Christmas Day. But too much work had taken its toll, and we were both sick the entire week. We went around town in the snowy weather, coughing with each other in syncopated rhythm. Eventually our coughing duet would give us a case of the giggles, which would start the coughing all over again. Great fun, and glamorous, too — we were a pair of real dolls.

Love always comes when you least expect it. One night Nicki and I were doped up on every cough medicine imaginable in an attempt to squelch the hacking and be socially acceptable. We wanted to go out on the town. At the Pioneer Saloon we got into a conversation with a delightful family who invited us to their home after dinner. Low and behold, the dad was divorced. He had so many qualities I liked. And his two adult children were mature, considerate, and a favorable reflection on their father. By the end of the evening I liked their dad a lot. And he took a liking to me.

John Reely and I spent as much time together as possible before we went our separate ways after the holiday. He returned to Arizona and I went home to California. Unlike most vacation romances though, this one continued after the vacation. He flew out to see me within two weeks. As I got to know him better, I saw someone who was living life the way I wanted to: He had a magical balance of work and responsibility combined with a sense of adventure. He emphasized sports and travel as much as he did work, yet his level of professional success was impressive.

When it comes to learning and growing, I believe in surrounding myself with people who already embody what I aspire to do. This is so I can learn by osmosis. John Reely was a model of adventure, discipline, organization, strength and integrity. He had taken some of life's hard knocks and dealt with them constructively. He was the kind of person who could challenge me to be the best I could be. All that, and attractive, too!

Some choices had to be made in order to conduct a romance from a thousand miles away. The television shows were the first thing to go. But I didn't mind. My original goal was to carve my life around my personal interests rather than around work. The news shows were too demanding and required too much preparation. They did not fit my goals.

I expanded the executive search work to include the biotechnology industry through a new friend, Leslie. With the TV work gone, I focused on apartment management and executive search work. Even that was a lot to handle. But I was then free to share adventures with John. He is passionate about travel.

As I met John in different travel destinations, I refined the logistics of taking work on the road. At the same time, my personal priorities expanded: I wanted to master the delicate balance of being productive and playing at the same time, just to see if I could do it. I was getting lots of practice since we met someplace different almost every month. It was a fun way to grow and learn.

If I were to pare down what I learned during that time to a few qualities important to successful work-travel, I would start with:

- **Fulfillment.** Get beyond survival and into a basic level of fulfillment. A fulfilled person is complete, in and of himself. A fulfilled person has health, a home, transportation, loving relationships, and the means to provide food and necessities. From a fulfilled state of mind, you can springboard into dreams that weren't possible before. My seemingly impossible desire for freedom and personal power began as a little girl fantasizing about Pegasus. It took me almost 50 years to get near that place of fulfillment. In my years raising a family as a "starving student," coping with Tara's situation, and lupus, there was no room to seek personal satisfaction. Survival was all I could hope for. Not until I learned the lessons from those chapters in my life was I able to move past survival issues into fulfillment. As a fulfilled person, I was free to create and pursue dreams, like having work that would travel.

Once survival issues are covered and there is a solid home, reliable transportation, good health, love, and monetary satisfaction, then you can look around to see what's next. But you will get no further, unless you cultivate some additional qualities:

- **Curiosity.** Without a desire to know what's around the corner, or how things could be better, stagnation will develop. Curiosity is driven by a desire for adventure. Curiosity feeds the willingness to take a risk to see what's on the other side. This does not guarantee happy endings. I have certainly made mistakes in my life as I have taken risks. But I have learned from each mistake, and have no regrets. As a result, I have the freedom to continue to be curious and have a sense of adventure.
- **Discipline.** There are times when I wish I weren't so serious. But I need serious discipline and strength to carry me through the steps needed to satisfy my curiosity. Discipline is the serious, flip-side of curiosity. Discipline is

what gets me to my goals, and to the fun, in style. Discipline exists on more than one level. By being disciplined about work, even when I'm in some wonderful location, I can then enjoy that special place for two, three or even six weeks at a time. On a grander scale, discipline and strength are required, without a doubt, to get through life's lessons, and move beyond survival, into a level of fulfillment.

- **Simplicity.** This is the wonderful lesson I learned from Tara: minimal motion for maximum effect. Have you ever noticed that people who are successful at what they do make it look easy? They have simplified. There is no excess bogging them down: They have room for peak levels of efficiency. This can also apply to simplifying material possessions. Paring down clears the mind and makes room for creativity.

I like to think that I will live to be 100 years old. Given what we now know about nutrition, exercise, medicine and so forth, 100 years of vital living is a reasonable expectation. So, why not take a risk? I refuse to be around people who say they are "too old" to do something, anything. I don't want that kind of thinking poisoning my own thoughts. If I'm 50 years old now, and have another 50 years to go, why not learn a new skill, start a new career, learn an exciting sport, explore a new continent?

With that kind of thinking comes liberation. "So what if I try and fail? I have another 50 years to make up for it." "So what if I don't have the skills. I have plenty of time to acquire them." "I have no desire to sit around repeating the same old lifestyle for another 50 years." *That's* the kind of thinking necessary to re-carve your life so that you can "have work will travel."

-6-

FORMULATE THE DREAM
Analyze personal strengths and weaknesses before launching —

So many people ask me "How do you do it?" Even in a beautiful destination resort town, where people make lifestyle choices to work and live there during the high season, they want to know "What kind of work do you do that allows you to bring it up here? How can I do that?" They'd like even more freedom than they already have for a summer season, or during ski season. They'd like work that they can take on the road to a variety of places, year-round.

Given the number of years I spent getting to this point, building a work-travel life is obviously a long-term plan. But it doesn't have to take 50 years to get here! And people with varied personality traits can do it. It's not a matter of repeating my life lessons or trying to develop my particular strengths. It's a matter of recognizing and tapping into your own set of talents. Every life story is unique and its lessons can be used to develop work that will travel. Any fulfilled individual can do it. Just be ready to simplify life's many options, and focus on combining work with the adventures you want to pursue.

There is no single way to carve out work that will travel. As you read about the numerous approaches to this lifestyle, you'll see many character traits that can benefit a "have work will travel" life. You'll also see a variety of stumbling blocks that can hold people back. While you're at it, turn the mirror on yourself. Your own strengths and weaknesses will begin to surface. Your strengths can be consciously used to attain your work-travel goals. As you move through the process, the journey itself is worthwhile on many levels.

For starters, having work that will travel can be a great lifestyle. It is full of new experiences, challenges and satisfaction, and can lead to a very well-rounded life. Boredom is not a factor here. The goal is to have the best of all worlds. And, you can end up with a greater appreciation of home at the same time.

I happen to like my current hometown, Phoenix, Arizona. But it gets *hot* there in the summer! So I take my work up to the mountains of Idaho for six weeks to cool off. While I'm there, I take some wonderful hikes and bike rides, and I travel through Canada, Montana, Wyoming and other beautiful places nearby. When I lived in beautiful San Francisco, I would escape during the crowded summer tourist season and go back when the city was returned to the locals. By leaving home when I like it least, I return with a heightened appreciation of what is special about where I live.

But is this nomadic life right for you? Let's assume you have honestly determined that you live a **fulfilled** life and your survival issues are being met. Let's also assume that you have searched your soul and feel that you are a **curious** individual, willing to take risks for the thrill of new experiences. And if it is inherent in you to be **disciplined** about important projects and goals, you are far along in the process.

We won't worry about **simplicity** yet. You can use your sense of fulfillment, curiosity and discipline to create simplicity. They will drive you to clarify your goals. Simplicity naturally follows.

If fulfillment, curiosity and discipline aren't part of your personal makeup, you might reexamine your desire to carry off a working-traveling life. A lack of any of these qualities would be a weakness that must be overcome. Your own level of desire will determine whether you can build these traits in yourself, or at least compensate for your weaknesses with other strengths.

Don't take my use of the word "weaknesses" personally. We all have them. The more familiar we are with our own weaknesses, the stronger we are. We can either change them or learn to compensate for what we cannot change. Knowing our weaknesses is probably more important than knowing our strengths.

Try this brief exercise. You'll discover your strengths and will start to know what work-and-travel tools are available to you. And, you will face your weaknesses head on:

1. Fold a piece of standard-size paper in half lengthwise.
2. Write "MY STRENGTHS" at the top of the left side of the paper.
3. Write "MY WEAKNESSES" at the top of the right side of the paper.
4. List your greatest assets on the "strengths" side. On the other side list what you consider your weakest traits.

Start by quickly listing what first comes to mind. Write as fast as you can. Review the list and tuck it into the back of this book. You'll be returning to it.

Keep thinking about your strengths and weaknesses, both in the present and in the past. Add to the list as you think of new ways to describe your personal qualities.

Take your time as you add to the list. Look back to your childhood. What were you especially good at? In what activities did you excel (sports, schoolwork, social activities, family interactions)? What recognition did you receive? What were your dreams and fantasies? What was difficult for you? On a separate piece of paper you might even want to write down some of these stories as your memories get rolling. It could be inspirational.

Next, review your life as a teenager and young adult making your first life decisions. It might give you more insight into your strengths and weaknesses. As you review your life, slowly graduate to the present and see if you have developed any new qualities worth noting.

Just to give you an idea, my own list looks like this:

MY STRENGTHS	MY WEAKNESSES
Organized & efficient	Physically weak (lupus)
Disciplined	Lazy
Not afraid to seek help	Self-critical
Like people – networking ability	Nervous & irritable when rushed
Persistent	Stubborn
Creatively solve problems	Impatient
Athletic	Intense
Solid business experience	Overly serious
Able to laugh at myself	Interrupt others in conversation
Adventurous	Lack of focus

I spent less than five minutes coming up with this list. I could add to it over time by reviewing my life from childhood to the present. With this short list in hand, I can assess which of these strengths are most important to my working and traveling life and which weaknesses hold me back.

On your own list:
1. Put a star next to the strengths that will most help you reach your work-travel goal.
2. Put a big dot next to weaknesses that could potentially keep you from reaching your goal.
3. Ask yourself: Can any of your starred strengths be used to retrain or compensate for any of your dotted weaknesses?
4. If so, draw a line from the strength to the weakness that can be

overcome by that strength. Begin a self-awareness campaign to reduce or eliminate the impact of each dotted weakness in your life.

For example, I compensate for being **lazy** by being **organized & efficient** and **disciplined.** With efficiency and discipline I get more accomplished in less time, and still have time left to indulge in my inherent laziness. These strengths also help me overcome being **physically weak** due to lupus, and my tendency to get **nervous and irritable when I am rushed.**

Being **able to laugh at myself** helps to overcome my **overly serious** nature. The serious, intense side of my personality is not likely to go away entirely, but I can mitigate it with a little humor at my own expense.

Lack of focus was a harder nut for me to crack. I finally came to terms with that weakness by embracing it. For example, I lacked focus when I started college. I began as a music major and thought I'd become a great violinist. But there were too many other things I wanted to pursue. So I was frustrated in my attempt to commit to the violin. I played the piano daily, designed and made all my clothes, read everything from Shakespeare to Vonnegutt, strove for good grades in school, and enjoyed a fun social life. I didn't want to give up any of that. But there wasn't enough time left for me to develop any level of greatness on the violin. So I changed my major to nutrition and pursued the arts as a hobby, instead of a career. That decision was very liberating for me.

I now know that I would rather *not* concentrate on any one thing enough to be great at it. Mediocrity may not be a virtue in some people's eyes, but I have the pleasure of enjoying a broad slice of life because I choose not to strive for perfection with a singular focus. I am happier when I mix it all up. The strengths I drew upon to deal with **lack of focus** have been to **creatively solve**

problems, and to indulge my **adventurous** side instead of demanding perfection in my activities.

Know your strengths and weaknesses. I cannot emphasize this enough. The same goes for *using* your strengths to offset weaknesses as you work toward your goals. I hope you will take the time to do the exercise. And please, continue to be aware of minimizing your weaknesses as you work toward having work that will travel. The awareness you gain will be invaluable in all aspects of your life.

I know this is all easier said than done, but as we explore the practical tactics for setting up a "have work will travel" life, I will share with you stories of various people I have observed. We'll spy on their lives and consider their strengths and weaknesses. Of course, names are embellished to protect the innocent.

Each of these individuals, by recognizing their weaknesses and learning to work around them, can work and travel if they choose. And they all have their own unique strengths to tap into. Hopefully you will recognize bits of yourself in some of their stories.

-7-

BE REALISTIC
Apply honesty during self-assessment, before making major decisions —

One of the biggest favors you can do for yourself is be honest when you assess your personal weaknesses and strengths. Be brutally honest. By truly facing your situation, you will save inestimable time, effort and heartache: You'll avoid barking up the wrong trees. And every step you take will be easier.

Be realistic about your self-discipline. Working and traveling is not for someone who needs assignments and deadlines imposed on them by someone else. You have to motivate yourself to stay with the program.

Are you afraid to stick your neck out and market yourself? This is not a job for the meek. Toot your own horn! Nobody but your own mother should speak more highly of your accomplishments than you do. And unless your mother is on your sales team, you have to sell yourself. Salesmanship is required, whether you are selling a boss on letting you work remotely, or whether you are selling your service to potential clients.

Are you afraid of hard work? Sometimes, as you transition into this lifestyle, you have to work two or more jobs at once until you phase in the new work-and-travel business. As I'll say often during the course of this book, **this takes a lot of dedication.**

How optimistic are you? This is very important. At every setback you need to re-boost your damaged ego, your momentum, and your creativity. You must see a problem as an opportunity to learn something new, or as a reason to come up with a better method.

Do you have the self-assurance to become a jack-of-all-trades? You may have to: Fix your own office equipment, gather your own resources, train and educate yourself, be a strategist, do your own accounting, motivate yourself, sell your services, and placate unhappy customers. If you feel unsure of yourself in any of these areas, you need confidence to jump-start your abilities in the weakest ones. You can learn any area of business where you are inexperienced — *if* you are bold enough to take it on.

My long-time friend, whom I'll call Denise the Dilettante, needed to work on building up all the traits I mentioned here: self-honesty, discipline, confidence, as well as update her business skills. This sounded like an awfully tall order. Let's review her situation and see how she conquered the problems.

Denise was 46 years old and had never drawn a paycheck in her life. She grew up in a ranching family in California. Many people would think that she married well because her husband was educated and wealthy. Denise admitted to a lack of confidence, which began early in her marriage. She felt inadequate without a college degree. But no one saw her lack of confidence at first glance because she was outgoing, articulate, thoughtful of others, and active in the community.

Denise spent her early adult years raising her family. She was also an advocate of charitable causes for the arts and for literacy. In her spare time, she honed her healthy good looks outdoors — skiing, riding horses, bicycling and keeping up with her children. She was an involved mother, and now takes great pride in how successful and productive her grown children have become.

So what was the problem? The problem was Denise's life of privilege. It sheltered her from everyday challenges that would have strengthened her for the difficulties she faced later. She did not experience the structure of the workday world. And she did not have role models who were goal-oriented self-starters.

When Denise Dilettante's marriage failed after 15 years, she had no foundation for starting a new, productive working life. She ended up with insufficient spousal support to live in the manner to which she had become accustomed. So she began looking at her choices. She had to either get creative with earning a living, or settle for a drastically reduced lifestyle. A third alternative would have been for Denise to pursue a long courtroom battle, but that would have led to a lot of negativity and possibly no improvement in her financial situation. Not an attractive option.

Denise chose to get creative with earning a living and bring in more income. She had a business idea that she could run from her house. She and a partner would combine talents in a fashion retail business. Denise had the fashion and purchasing know-how, and her partner had the business acumen. She was excited that the plan would allow her the freedom to travel. But now that she wanted to carve a life of independence, she came up against her own barriers.

The new business would take some concentrated effort to get up and running. And Denise had trouble setting aside the time to get started. She still felt the need to raise money for the opera, symphony and ballet, plus read to homeless children. She scattered valuable time throughout each week, adding up to 20 or more fragmented hours of volunteerism — detracting from her goals. Also, friends and family came in and out of the house all week, or called her on the phone day and night. They demanded attention when she was trying to work on her business idea.

Denise's old feeling of inadequacy at having no college degree still haunted her. She also expected endless hours of perfect solitude to concentrate. She was reluctant to start until that Utopian environment was there. To make things worse, she spent more time reading how-to books than she spent doing what she learned from the books.

If Denise Dilettante sat down and wrote a short list of the strengths and weaknesses at play in her life, it might look like this:

STRENGTHS	WEAKNESSES
Dedicated volunteer	Lack of formal degree or work experience
Outgoing personality	Disorganized
Well-spoken	Too many activities
Good connections to people in business	Too many excuses
Excellent written skills	Negative thinker
Self-taught computer skills	Lack of confidence
Broad life experiences	Procrastinator
Excellent fundraiser	Distracted by friends & family

So how did Denise play down her weaknesses to enable her to build her "have work will travel" business?

She started by using her **excellent written skills** to attack **disorganization** and having too many activities. The first thing she wrote was a list of the plusses and minuses of her involvement with each charitable cause. Her lists revealed which activities needed to go, and which single cause was most inspiring. That made it easier to make the hard choices — cutting out all except the most valued aspects of her favorite charity. She freed up time and added the **simplicity** she needed. The end result was more satisfying because she contributed to the community in a more focused manner.

Her next written piece was a résumé emphasizing the valuable skills she had learned as a **dedicated volunteer** including sales (as an **excellent fundraiser**), public speaking, computer abilities, distinctive accomplishments, and numerous organizing skills. This alone was a boost to her. Soon her **lack of confidence** and **negative thinking** about her **lack of formal degree or work experience** diminished.

She then used her **well-spoken** qualities on the phone to arrange face-to-face meetings with people she knew in the fashion world and with potential customers. This also used her **outgoing personality** and **good connections to people in business.** By meeting first with people she already knew, she got a positive response, which reinforced her confidence right off the bat. As she made progress toward her goals, she was less inclined to come up with **too many excuses.**

By telling others about her plan, Denise Dilettante also fended off her **procrastinator** tendency. For one thing, her business idea seemed more tangible when she shared it. It would be embarrassing for Denise if others asked her how it was going, and it was going nowhere. So it was a sort of backhanded form of motivation.

When she told others about her plan, she also informed them of her new in-home office hours. That gave her the opportunity to tell them in advance that she wouldn't be taking visitors or personal phone calls during that time. By enforcing her office hours, she would no longer be **distracted by friends and family.**

These were just Denise Dilettante's initial baby steps. She will be able to use her strengths throughout the entire growth of her business. When she examines herself even more closely, she will find additional assets she can draw upon as she continues on her path.

Denise Dilettante already has a **fulfilled** life. Her spousal support allows her to move well beyond the survival issues of transportation, home, food and clothing. She also has the **curiosity** to expand her level of fulfillment, and experience new challenges for herself. She has enough solid strengths that she can develop the **discipline** she needs, if her desire to succeed is strong. She is past the planning stage of her business right now, and has begun buying inventory. Before long, her name just might have to change to Denise the Dynamo as she becomes more accomplished.

Had Denise refused to face her demons, we'd have a different story. If she had pulled the wool over her eyes rather than honestly examining her weaknesses, she would still be caught in a vicious cycle of chaos, excuses and insecurity. Instead she is moving toward simplicity, solutions and confidence.

If you have not already listed your own strengths and weaknesses, I recommend that you take the time to go back to that step. Refer to pages 56-59 in Chapter 6, "Formulate the Dream." Take your time thinking about your personal qualities and how they impact your life. Once you take stock you can move forward with purpose, knowing your capabilities.

-8-

MONETARY PROS AND CONS
Look at financial aspects of a "have work will travel" life —

There is a price to pay for the benefits received from any worthwhile endeavor. For some people, the price of freedom and a "have work will travel" life is too high. As for me, I'm happy to pay the price for that freedom. I'm just plain wired to want freedom. Each individual needs to honestly assess whether this is the life for him or her. Do the pros outweigh the cons? Let's take a look at some important factors to include in the equation.

In most cases you will not have the security of a regular paycheck. If you have worked your entire life for a weekly, bi-weekly, or monthly paycheck, take a close look at the idea of something less secure. Remember, as you think about this, there is also the possibility of earning *more* than you ever earned in that paycheck. You are no longer bound to the limitations set by an employer. The possible negative aspect of no regular paycheck just might be offset by the unlimited potential to earn more than that paycheck could ever be. Be brutally honest. Can you handle stepping off the cliff, not knowing which way it will go?

Once a working-traveling life is created, work takes place from two primary locations. One is a home-based location, usually an office or studio in the home. The second is a travel destination, which will vary from trip to trip.

As you set financial and performance goals, keep in mind that by working at home, or as you travel, you can save a lot of money in daily expenses. When you travel to work every day for an employer, the costs add up. You should calculate the potential savings from changing your work structure. The savings could be large enough to be a pivotal factor in your decision. Realistically assess your costs for commuting, dry cleaning, restaurant or café lunches, midday cappuccinos, fast-food dinners after work, child care, and payroll deductions for a start. And you might even be able to get rid of an extra car, or make other suitable reductions if you work at home and while traveling.

Plus, many expenses you incur as an employee are not tax deductible for you. If you implement your plan to "have work will travel" as a self-employed individual, almost every business expense you incur will be deductible. Either check with an accountant or chat with a friend who is self-employed. They can give you guidelines on the tax benefits to expect.

On the downside, there are usually a lot of expenses to budget in when you have work that will travel. Sometimes these costs are sizable. Business expenses vary drastically from one kind of work to another. And travel expenses will be even more diverse from one person to the next.

If you already spend a lot on vacation travel, your travel costs might not be higher than before. If you have not traveled much until now, you must factor in the costs of your travel. In some cases it will be tax deductible as part of your business. In other cases, travel is a personal expense that you will have to "eat," so to speak. Since there are many ways to travel, ranging from lavish to bare bones, you can fit your travel-style to your budget. How you approach it will depend on the income you generate, and on your personal tastes in travel. When I was living on an extremely tight budget, I did road trips and stayed with friends. Camping is another option on a tight budget, depending on your work needs when you travel.

Another possibility is to do a house trade when you travel. This can be done with people you know in other areas, or there are house exchange services that provide lists of homes available. They can add your house or apartment to their list for a nominal charge. Just match your needs with someone in another part of the U.S., or another country. There are people who want to trade for a week or a couple of months. And don't worry about your home being inadequate: For many people the idea of a tiny apartment in a place they want to visit is far superior to an expensive and impersonal motel room.

Go to your favorite bookstore and scan the travel section. There will be books that inspire you to new adventures. At the same time ferret out the books that include tips on doing house exchanges. Evaluate carefully whether this is an option for you. If it is, some of those books will provide contact information for listing services. You can also access these services by running a search for "house exchanges" on the Internet. They are sort of like matchmaking services for dating, with the same potential for success or failure. So go in with your eyes wide open.

When you have work that will travel, there are also nuts-and-bolts expenses to take into account. I go into detail on travel equipment and service needs in Chapters 11 through 15. Estimate your preliminary equipment needs. Think about costs such as long distance and Internet services, business checking accounts, and accounting or tax software. These can be partially offset by taking advantage of tax deductions and depreciating equipment expenses on your tax returns. Tax benefits plus money saved from avoiding the commuting life might just make working and traveling look attractive. Every situation will be different.

For now you probably have not done a formal business

plan. While I highly recommend that you do one, business plans are not part of the focus of this book. But at least do some mental calculating. For example, on pages 72-76 and in the back of the book, Addendum I, you will find work sheets you can photocopy for your calculations. Here is a summary of how they work:

- Add up how much you'll save in commuting expenses, paycheck withholdings, etc., by changing your work situation. For this example, let's plug in a figure of $800 per month in savings.
- Subtract from that figure the additional costs of equipment and increased phone services, etc. Get an IRS Tax Form 1040 "Schedule C" to see what expense categories might apply to you. For our example, we'll assume office expenses and other estimated costs will be about $650 per month beyond what you spent when you worked for a paycheck.
- Add in estimated income tax savings from any business deductions you could not take before. If you think you might save $2,000 per year in taxes, that is a savings of $167 per month.
- Subtract the larger self-employment tax (Social Security and Medicare contributions) you are likely to pay. At the time of this writing, self-employment tax is usually double that of an employee's withholdings for Social Security and Medicare. That is because as an employee you pay only half of these withholdings — your employer pays the other half. Let's say, as an employee, you now contribute $66.50 for these items. In your self-employed role, if your net earnings were about the same as your current salary, you'd pay an *additional* $66.50 per month. Your tax consultant can help you calculate estimated

self-employment tax.

The rules change constantly on all tax-related issues. **Check with a tax advisor for accurate information related to your own situation.**

- The basic math for the above example looks like this:

    $ 800.00 per month you save by not commuting, etc.
    − 650.00 monthly expense for equipment, phone, supplies, etc.
    + 167.00 tax savings while self-employed
    <u>− 66.50 additional self-employment tax (Social Security/Medicare)</u>
    $250.50 saved each month by working for yourself

According to this scenario, you save $250.50 per month by working at home or on the road. That $250.50 could be put into your travel budget. Or apply it to a financial cushion for emergencies. Not everyone's preliminary math will be so positive. Please be realistic at this stage.

In this example, if your income was about the same after you shifted to working and traveling, then you would actually improve your situation by working at home. The big unknown is whether you can continue to earn as much. That will depend on what you decide to do as a business (see Chapter 10 "Put the Dream into Action"). It also depends on how effectively you prepare and market your business.

If your own numbers result in a negative figure, and it would cost more for you to work at home than work for someone else, now is the time to face that issue. It doesn't rule out having work that will travel. It does mean you need to adjust a few of your ideas. You can uncover more cost-efficient ways to manage your business or explore how you might make even more money than before. What about downsizing your current housing and lifestyle to fit your new "have work will travel" life? But again, be brutally honest about your potential before you give up a good job for work and travel.

Now is the time to plug in your own numbers to see how your situation looks. They are your *preliminary* numbers to use as a reality check. Figures may change as you learn more, so make more than one copy of the work sheets and try different scenarios.

I have deliberately left out recreational travel expenses: They vary so much depending on how often and how expensively you go. Travel is where you have the most control over costs. **Set your travel budget *after* you do your final business budget. Then revise travel plans upward or downward as needed.**

WORK SHEET
MONETARY SAVINGS AND COSTS

STEP 1. SAVINGS

Current work expenses that you would *no longer* incur if you stopped working at an employer's site:

Activity	Per Day	Work Days/Month	Savings/Month
Commute by car, bus etc.	$____	x _____	= $____
Dry cleaning	$____	x _____	= $____
Lunches out	$____	x _____	= $____
Breakfasts out	$____	x _____	= $____
Coffee & latte breaks	$____	x _____	= $____
Fast-food dinners	$____	x _____	= $____
Child care	$____	x _____	= $____
Misc. payroll deductions	$____	x _____	= $____
Other	$____	x _____	= $____
Other	$____	x _____	= $____

Can you sell an extra car? For how much?
  Divide that number by 12 = $_____
Add up all expenses in the "Savings/Month" row.
  TOTAL SAVED = $_____

STEP 2. EXPENDITURES

Estimate your costs to run a business from home and travel destinations. Include only the costs *above and beyond* your current situation:

Estimated Expense	Per Year	Per Month
Advertising	$_____	÷ 12 = $_____
Accounting & tax preparation	$_____	÷ 12 = $_____
Car and truck expense	$_____	÷ 12 = $_____
Education	$_____	÷ 12 = $_____
Equipment (computer, cell phone, fax, etc.)	$_____	÷ 12 = $_____
Office expense	$_____	÷ 12 = $_____
Insurance	$_____	÷ 12 = $_____
Interest expense	$_____	÷ 12 = $_____
Legal and professional services	$_____	÷ 12 = $_____
Repairs and maintenance	$_____	÷ 12 = $_____
Supplies	$_____	÷ 12 = $_____
Licenses	$_____	÷ 12 = $_____
Business travel	$_____	÷ 12 = $_____
Meals and entertainment	$_____	÷ 12 = $_____
Utilities (phone service, Internet fees, etc.)	$_____	÷ 12 = $_____
Other	$_____	÷ 12 = $_____
Other	$_____	÷ 12 = $_____

Total estimated expenses in the Per Month column for:

TOTAL SPENT = $_____

STEP 3. TAX SAVINGS

Your TOTAL SPENT column roughly mirrors what your tax-deductible items would be working for yourself. There will be variations, so always consult a tax professional before making final decisions. But for now, we are just estimating. Next, we will find out your estimated tax savings from self-employment. Multiply your TOTAL SPENT (from Step 2 on page 73) by your estimated tax rate. If you are unsure of your tax rate, check with your tax consultant. Or, for the sake of this illustration, plug in 25% to get an idea. We are used to thinking of taxes in annual amounts. But since we are dealing with monthly amounts so far, let's continue to get a monthly tax savings. So:

TOTAL SPENT $_____ x ___ % = **TAX SAVINGS** of $_____ per mo.
Your tax rate or 25%

STEP 4. SELF-EMPLOYMENT TAX (SOCIAL SECURITY)

Current self-employment tax is 15.3% of your net earnings (if under $7,075 per month). **This could change. Check with your tax advisor.** Estimate the gross income you expect to earn. From gross income subtract your TOTAL SPENT to get net earnings. Multiply net earnings by 15.3%, or the number provided by your tax advisor, to estimate your self-employment tax. Divide that by two, because when you are employed, your employer pays half. You then have an idea of how much *extra* Social Security and Medicare you'll contribute. It will look like this:

EST. GROSS INCOME per month: $ _____
   (your own estimate)

Minus: **TOTAL SPENT** − _____
   (from page 73)

Equals: **APPROX. NET EARNINGS** = _____

Times: **SELF-EMPLOYMENT TAX RATE** x _____ %
   (15.3% or % from tax advisor)

Equals: **TOTAL SELF-EMPLOYMENT TAX** = _____

Divide by 2: **SELF-EMPLOYMENT TAX** ÷ 2 = _____
   extra tax you pay if you are self-employed

STEP 5. TOTAL MONEY SAVED EACH MONTH

To get your end result, do the following math:

Enter:	**TOTAL SAVED**	= $_____	(from page 72)
Minus:	**TOTAL SPENT**	− $_____	(from page 73)
Plus:	**TAX SAVINGS**	+ $_____	(from page 74)
Minus:	**SELF-EMPLOYMENT TAX**	− $_____	(from page 75)
Equals:	**MONEY SAVED**	= $_____	each month you work for yourself

If you have a negative figure in the MONEY SAVED total, then it would cost you more to work at home/traveling than to stay in your current situation. Now is the time to review your figures. See where you can cut costs to make it work.

As you go further into this book you'll revise your numbers when you get new ideas about equipment, services, and consolidating expenses. There is a fresh work sheet like this one in Addendum I. Make multiple copies so you can try various scenarios. These numbers are important in your decision-making process.

Remember that some, possibly all, of your business equipment needs might be met with equipment you now use for your personal life such as: cell phone, home fax or answering machine, voice mail, etc. Think frugally and try to use what you already have.

There is a fine line that you must walk as you analyze the monetary pros and cons of having work that will travel. If you naively look at everything on the bright side, you could get in real trouble by ignoring pitfalls. Yet, if your attitude is too negative, you risk talking yourself out of what could be an exciting and profitable opportunity.

My friend Darrel the Devil's Advocate loves this kind of

analysis. In fact, he's so good at it, he talks himself out of almost every opportunity that comes his way. But he is successfully living the "have work will travel" life, so we can learn from him.

Darrel the Devil's Advocate grew up in a household that valued education. He went to prestigious schools and earned a bachelor's degree in engineering and a master's in business. He has the basic tools to succeed in the business world. He started his adult life working for a regular paycheck in the construction industry.

Darrel married his college sweetheart. While they were raising their children, he invested wisely. After only a few years' experience in the work-a-day world, he left the daily grind to run his own construction projects, funded by the money he had cultivated. Darrel and his family were also able to ski in Europe, take cruises, and travel almost anywhere they chose. While he played with his family, he was fanatical about checking his phone messages and maintaining his business responsibilities, no matter how expensive the international phone bills ran.

Things were going swimmingly for Darrel until about 20 years into his marriage when his wife decided to call it quits. Suddenly, his investment cushion was cut in half. Darrel's newly reduced equities would not support his former lifestyle for very long. A change in strategy was in order.

Darrel had the wisdom to take his time reinvesting, to maximize income and minimize risk. He pursued ventures conservatively and spent years deciding on the right business that would provide sufficient income to allow him to travel.

But Darrel the Devil's Advocate became so negative in his assessment of potential ventures that he paralyzed his ability to act. He admits he has turned down sensible opportunities because he analyzed them to death. When he looks back on missed opportunities, hindsight shows that some of them were viable. He would now be more financially successful if he had moved forward with a few of those ventures.

Now, let's not feel too sorry for Darrel. He still travels to exotic places and pursues exciting sports. He has to monitor every penny wherever he goes — but he goes! Because his income is smaller now, he had to settle for a smaller house and concede a few other luxuries. We'll learn a lot from the strengths and weaknesses he would list. He is inspiring. A life of conservative, knowledgeable investing, with mindful attention to the details of running the business, can support a "have work will travel" life.

Darrel would most likely list his attributes and flaws as follows:

STRENGTHS	WEAKNESSES
Frugal	See problems instead of solutions
Experienced in business	A worry-wart
Good business contacts	Lack confidence
Detail oriented	Not tactful when dealing with people
Sense of adventure	Critical of others
Organized	Lonely

Darrel the Devil's Advocate has a lot of attributes to work with, if he can get past his negative attitude. He can expose himself to ongoing business ventures by way of his **good business contacts.** All he has to do is compensate for his negativity, which takes the form of being **critical**, a **worry-wart**, and **seeing problems instead of solutions**. Since he is aware of these drawbacks, he is far along in the process.

He might even use his **experience** and **good business contacts** to seek out a well-chosen business partner. A partner who appeals to Darrel's common-sense approach, yet counters Darrel's negativity would be a good choice. Someone who may be younger, hard-working, reliable, and eager to gain experience would be ideal. That person would also need to be inherently optimistic and upbeat in order to compensate for Darrel's innate critical ways. An upbeat partner could encourage Darrel to look more favorably on business ventures. And a partnership could alleviate some of Darrel's sense of being **lonely**.

Darrel the Devil's Advocate might have to split the pie with a partner, but the pie would most likely be bigger because Darrel could accept opportunities to expand more readily. There could be more for everyone.

-9-

LIFESTYLE PROS AND CONS
There are social issues to consider, plus the value of time —

Another aspect to consider when you evaluate cost savings vs. cost increases is the value of your time. How long do you spend commuting now? And, before you head out the door, how many minutes are you primping to prepare yourself for the outside world? Now honestly assess the use of your time once you are at work. How much time do you spend gabbing with co-workers about non-work issues? Do you also spend time in meetings that feel like a waste of time? If so, how much time each week? I wouldn't be surprised if your results looked something like this:

- Commute – 40 minutes door-to-door each way for a total of 80 minutes a day, which equals 6 2/3 hours per week
- Vanity – Men might spend 20 minutes each morning on vanity issues that they would ignore if they were not working outside the home. Women often spend much more and should increase the estimate accordingly. But, for our example, 20 minutes a day equals 1 2/3 hours per week.
- Office Banter – This includes the time you typically spend at the water cooler, attending office birthday parties, or recommending a repairman to a co-worker. That's what, maybe 30 minutes a day in distracting banter? I actually think I'm being very conservative here, and that

adds up to 2 1/2 hours a week of wasted time in the office.

• Office Meetings – If you only attend a single one-hour meeting a week that you feel is a waste of time, you're lucky. Many people find unnecessary meetings to be their biggest pet peeve at the office. But let's say it's only one hour per week: It's still a lot of time.

So, how do all of these time-wasters add up? They total a whopping 11 to 12 hours of non-productive time per week! And I truly think I'm being conservative here. Working for yourself at home or at a travel destination could add 11, 12 or more productive hours to your week.

The time saved by having work that travels can be viewed in terms of monetary savings to you. If you value your time at $25 per hour, you would add almost $300 per week to your income by applying your time more effectively. Here's another way to look at it: Some of this 11 to 12 hours of time per week could be reinvested in travel time, going to interesting destinations and working from there.

Let's take a closer look at how your time-wasters stack up. Use the blank work sheet right here. Or photocopy Addendum II at the back of the book to use as a work sheet.

Elizabeth Scott

WORK SHEET
TIME-WASTERS IN THE WORKPLACE

STEP 1.

Time-Waster Activity	Daily (In Minutes)	Days/Week (That You Work)	Weekly (In Minutes)	Converted to Hours (Per Week Wasted)
Commute (door-to-door, round trip)	____ x	____ =	____ ÷ 60 min. =	____ hrs.
Vanity (extra maintenance for skin, hair, face & clothing)	____ x	____ =	____ ÷ 60 min. =	____ hrs.
Office banter (be honest now)	____ x	____ =	____ ÷ 60 min. =	____ hrs.
Office meetings (the ones that didn't accomplish a thing)	____ x	____ =	____ ÷ 60 min. =	____ hrs.

Enter the total in the final space to get the hours per month you could save by working in a home-based travel situation

TOTAL HOURS _____
WASTED EACH WEEK

TOTAL HOURS x 4 = _____
WASTED EACH MONTH

STEP 2.

What hourly rate would you charge if you worked for yourself? Multiply that hourly rate by the TOTAL HOURS WASTED EACH MONTH (on the previous page). This determines the monetary value of the time you'd save working and traveling vs. working in a traditional environment.

$_____ your hourly rate x _____ **HOURS WASTED** = ____ **MONEY SAVED**
                                       EACH MONTH   **EACH MONTH**
                                                              by applying time
                                                              more effectively

---

WORK SHEET
THE GRAND TOTAL OF MONETARY SAVINGS
BY WORKING IN A NON-TRADITIONAL ENVIRONMENT

Now you can see the whole picture. There are two factors that decide whether you will save money by having work that will travel. One factor is actual monies saved, and the other factor is the value of time saved when you no longer work in a traditional environment. To come up with a single figure that represents the total you will:

Enter your final total from Step 5 on page 76, "Monetary Savings and Costs" Work Sheet:
     MONEY SAVED: $ _____

Add in your final total from this page, above, the "Time-Wasters in the Workplace" Work Sheet:
   MONEY SAVED EACH MONTH: $ _____

This equals your total savings by working at home and traveling:
     GRAND TOTAL: $ _____

A positive GRAND TOTAL means that it will probably be cost effective for you to work at home or while traveling.

A negative GRAND TOTAL means that it might not be cost effective for you to make a change in your work situation. Don't give up. Go back and see where you can trim costs. Or think of ways to boost your income in your new situation.

Even if you ended up saving quite a bit of money each month on your work sheet, you have a lot of other work conditions, besides cost savings, to take into account. Look closely at different aspects of giving up your employer's work situation. If you thrive on those water cooler conversations and office parties, give careful consideration to the potential for loneliness working on your own. Tell yourself the truth here. Can you isolate yourself from the office banter? Do you need to see human faces all day, each day, to be happy? Many people do need this contact, so don't beat yourself up about it if you need it, too. Now is the time to give it some thought.

If you determine that you really need a lot of human interaction each day, there are some possible alternatives to office-based work. These may allow you to work on your own and still enjoy quality people-time:

1. Get involved in your community after work. Volunteer at the local animal shelter (you get to interact with animals as well as people). Or join a political organization that fits your philosophy. Get involved with an environmental cause like the Sierra Club, which also hosts social events. Or begin fundraising for a favorite charity. Would that be enough socialization to satisfy your daily need?

2. Patronize a neighborhood restaurant or pub one or two times a week. Happy hour at the end of the day can be invigorating. You might meet new people who work near you, or you could

befriend the restaurant staff. The caution here is moderation in the drinking department. Imbibing on work nights could turn into a very bad habit. If you think you'd have that tendency, don't even attempt this solution unless you can stick to juices and sodas.

3. Start a book club, bridge club or investment club. An even easier way would be to join an existing one. You can learn a lot, stimulate your mind, and enjoy camaraderie with like-minded individuals.

4. Get physical. Join a baseball, basketball or volleyball league after work. Gather a group together for regular bowling. Or join a gym. When you're at the gym, check out the classes in aerobics, weights, kickboxing, Pilates, or whatever the latest trend-of-the-week may be in fitness. Participating in a class setting is a great way to meet people.

5. Take a couple of night classes. Anything from accounting to ceramics. Do what you enjoy, and it will put you in touch with people you'll like to be around.

6. Explore group travel options. Some museums coordinate fascinating trips to Asia, Africa or other areas of interest to the museum. Even high-end wine shops sponsor food and wine tours in France, Australia, California or other great wine regions. The Sierra Club and REI sports stores put together some exciting outdoor adventures. There are many entities that plan fascinating group trips, so you need not travel alone. Once you tune into the possibilities, you'll see that they are endless.

I could go on and on with ideas for socializing after work. The idea is that by working alone, you can work uninterrupted and be very effective with your time. Save your people-time for after-hours. Just match your own need for social stimulation to activities that come closest to satisfying your need.

If you are a working parent, there are many issues to

consider related to your family. Combining work, travel and parenting is a major juggling act. But if you are a parent, you are already doing a juggling act, right? Ask yourself whether you want to juggle even more balls by adding a home-based business or travel to the mix. If the answer is "yes, it would be worth it," then take a close look at your situation. Start creating solutions for each limitation you see.

Can you really work with youngsters underfoot? If they are in school, structuring your work time around school hours is the obvious solution. If they are too young for school, can you afford day care? What you do on their sick days and vacation days is yet another matter. If your work requires uninterrupted concentration, you will need to figure out how to isolate yourself when the kids are with you. Some jobs can continue in spite of constant interruptions. And some more flexible work, can grind to a halt when children's needs must come first, and be picked up again later.

As a working parent you will want to choose wisely when you decide on a business that will allow you to work, travel *and* parent. A few of the possibilities from Chapter 10, page 100, in the "Work That Fits" section, are secretarial service, phone sales, bookkeeping, real estate investment, and mail marketing. Use your imagination. Think of what you are good at and enjoy. Then it will be a lot easier to muster the extra dedication you'll need to accomplish your goals while keeping your family life intact.

Singles and couples both have relationship issues to consider. When one person is working and traveling, and the significant other is tied to one place, it's a challenge. And singles who seek a relationship sometimes have trouble making a meaningful connection when they travel a lot. The pros and cons of relationship issues need to be addressed.

There are four obvious relationship scenarios here:

1. Single and looking for Mr. or Ms. Right.
2. Single and happy to stay that way.
3. Coupled and one person is not free to travel.
4. Coupled and both people are free to work and travel.

As soon as you add another person to your life in a serious relationship, your choices must take that relationship into account unless you want to risk losing the other person. So give this a lot of thought as you carve your work-travel life. "Single and happy to stay that way" is obviously the easiest lifestyle to work with. But it is not the relationship choice for everyone.

If you are "single and looking," finding someone who can travel a lot is not as easy as it sounds. When you meet someone with relationship potential, exchange attitudes about travel with them early in the dating phase. How much do they like to travel? How much are they free to travel? If they are not free to travel, are they happy enough with their personal hobbies to be willing to stay at home alone? Just as important, are you willing to travel without the other person if need be?

Cleo the Corporate Climber is single and looking for Mr. Right. She has ambition, and loves corporate life. However, she is beginning to see that she wants a more rounded life, with flexible work hours and freedom to travel, along with a quality relationship. She has a good handle on how to set up and run a consulting business that would allow her to travel. For her, the biggest challenge will be to meet someone within her usual corporate circle who could blend in, in some way, with her desire to travel.

Cleo has met an attorney, Gary Golfer, at the wine bar near her office. He fits her life in so many ways. But his private practice doesn't allow him to pick up and go in the way she wants to travel. How can they work this out?

Well, it takes some rather modern thinking, relationshipwise.

But it can be done. If they have mutual trust and self-confidence, they can independently pursue their interests. Cleo's start-up business will be demanding at first. Add to that her desire to travel, and she can't be very attentive to Gary Golfer.

From Gary Golfer's perspective, Cleo is a breath of fresh air. His past girlfriends complained about being "golf widows" and tried to make him feel guilty about his passion for putting. Now that he is seeing Cleo the Corporate Climber, he enjoys guilt-free golf while she works overtime. So he feels satisfied and puts more energy into the time they do have together. Also when Cleo takes a trip that he really doesn't want to take, he goes on a golfing binge with no one nagging in the background.

Cleo has several girlfriends who like to travel. They plan trips together and Cleo gets the companionship she wants on her journeys. Since Cleo and Gary are both happy with this arrangement, it has the potential to work over the long haul.

Beware, though; not everyone has the capacity for so much independence. If you and your partner want to spend most of your time together, you might reassess your desire to have work that will travel. It could jeopardize the relationship.

Another couple, Judy Judge and Reggie Real Estate are both free to "have work will travel." Each of them has a passion for travel and has creatively carved work-travel lives for themselves. At first they had trouble competing for phone lines and computer time, arguing over limited resources on the road. But over time they have worked out those relatively minor details with separate cell phones and separate laptops. Now they travel merrily on their way to various parts of the U.S. and around the world.

There is another area where dedication and discipline are required to work and travel. I call it "life's daily needs." Life's daily needs rear their ugly heads and threaten to destroy work concentration all day, every day. One of life's daily needs demands attention, so you attend to something personal. But it's never enough. There is always another banking snafu, phone company error, grocery list to be filled, and on and on. Entire days can be eaten up by life's daily needs. Tap into your discipline and pace these greedy little chores. Don't let them eat your workday alive. Handle one thing at a time, and get right back to work. Be your own boss. Muster up your own discipline.

On another personal note, are you a night or a morning person? What is your optimal time of day? What time of day is best for you to schedule errands, exercise and other necessities? By living the work and travel life, you have freedom to maximize your scheduling. Just remember that discipline is required to pull yourself back into work mode each time you take a break. Once you have no boss looking over your shoulder, you have to monitor your own activities.

I happen to like the flexibility of working late into the evening and sleeping in the next morning. In the quiet of the night I am most productive. No phone calls, no interruptions. My focus is at its best. Then I relish the luxury of sleeping till 9:30 in the morning, guilt-free.

Right after breakfast I hit the home office and do banking chores on the computer, check e-mail, make phone calls, and get other busywork out of the way. Then I concentrate and do my most productive work without nagging details in the back of my mind. I get a midday boost if I take a break at around two in the afternoon to run to the gym, buy groceries, or other chores. This is a great time of day for me because the majority of the working world is still working. I don't wait in lines or deal with commuter crowds and traffic. Once I return and get back into creative mode I am at my best until as late as midnight, taking just one more break for dinner.

Your biorhythms might be different. You might be an early bird, up at dawn and ready to go. You can get some great quality time in the wee hours of the morning, just like I get late at night.

Discipline and dedication also apply when taking breaks during the day to fuel your energy. Keep the breaks short! This is a challenge. All of a sudden there is no boss glancing at his watch when you return, or looking over your shoulder to check on your production. You have to take on that role yourself.

Here's a test of your current level of self-discipline: How are you on weekends, or other off-work time in your life? Do you check off the chores on your list with satisfaction? Or do they get moved to next weekend? And then the weekend after that? If you are a procrastinator by nature, or if you tend to get overextended, juggling too many balls at one time, you have major work to do on yourself before giving up a day job that has built-in discipline enforced by someone else.

Francine Frantic has this problem. She extends herself in so many directions that she can't keep track of her highest priority projects. Important tasks are done late, or not at all. She races through life creating lots of motion with her part-time job in an insurance company and her involvement in her husband's trucking and storage business. In addition they have started a catering business and gift shop in one of their picturesque downtown buildings. She is a gal who works hard and plays hard. She doesn't want to miss out on a thing and is closely involved with her children's activities. She is also out at night visiting friends, diving into community affairs, and so on.

While Francine works very hard, she has become less effective in each endeavor because she lacks dedication and discipline in any single area. She is late submitting catering bids and misses out on jobs she could have won. She attends dinner parties two hours late because she worked at the store. Her family sees her as a flash out the door. The one area where she is prompt, and at maximum production, is the insurance company. There she has a boss watching the clock as she walks in the door. But sadly, the insurance company is what she wants to move out of, so she can help build her husband's business and expand her store and catering. There are some misplaced priorities here that can be realigned, with a little planning.

Francine would see her strengths and weaknesses as:

STRENGTHS	WEAKNESSES
Smart	Forgetful
Hardworking	Lack of focus
Outgoing	Harried
Loyal friend	Overwhelmed
Motivates others	Often late
Energetic	Lack of follow-up
Talented	Disorganized
Resourceful	Micro-manager

Francine's weaknesses all revolve around her **lack of focus**, giving her just one major issue to deal with. But for her it is a big one. Luckily she has many strengths to put to the task.

Francine is a **loyal** friend to many. With that loyalty she has **motivated others** to join in her ventures. If she learns to delegate to those who have worked alongside her in catering ventures, and in the store, she will be much less **harried**, far less **disorganized** and will be less of a **micro-manager.** She can delegate bookkeeping, scheduling floor time at the store and other tasks, to someone organized and trustworthy. Francine's loyalty to others over the years has generated many people in her life who are both organized and trustworthy.

Once she delegates some of the detail work, Francine will be far less **overwhelmed.** As she eliminates details, she'll see the big picture. She'll become effective at submitting bids, marketing, and managing the overall business plan. She can finally put her **talent** and **resourcefulness** to work. As she wins more lucrative catering jobs and the store gets more publicity, the cash flow will follow. At that point she can consider leaving her part-time insurance job and her **lack of focus** will be reduced.

As Francine grows confident in her ability to let go and delegate, she'll be able to travel as well. The family businesses are cyclical. Winter is quiet for the trucking business and the store. This means she can take some great winter trips, checking in from the road to ensure that things run well.

Francine Frantic has the energy and **curiosity** to go beyond basic **fulfillment** at the insurance company and seek a more adventurous life. She has the ability to delegate to others who have more sense of **organization.** Once the efficiency level increases in her business endeavors, she will also have the **simplicity** she needs to shift to a "have work will travel" life.

Developing

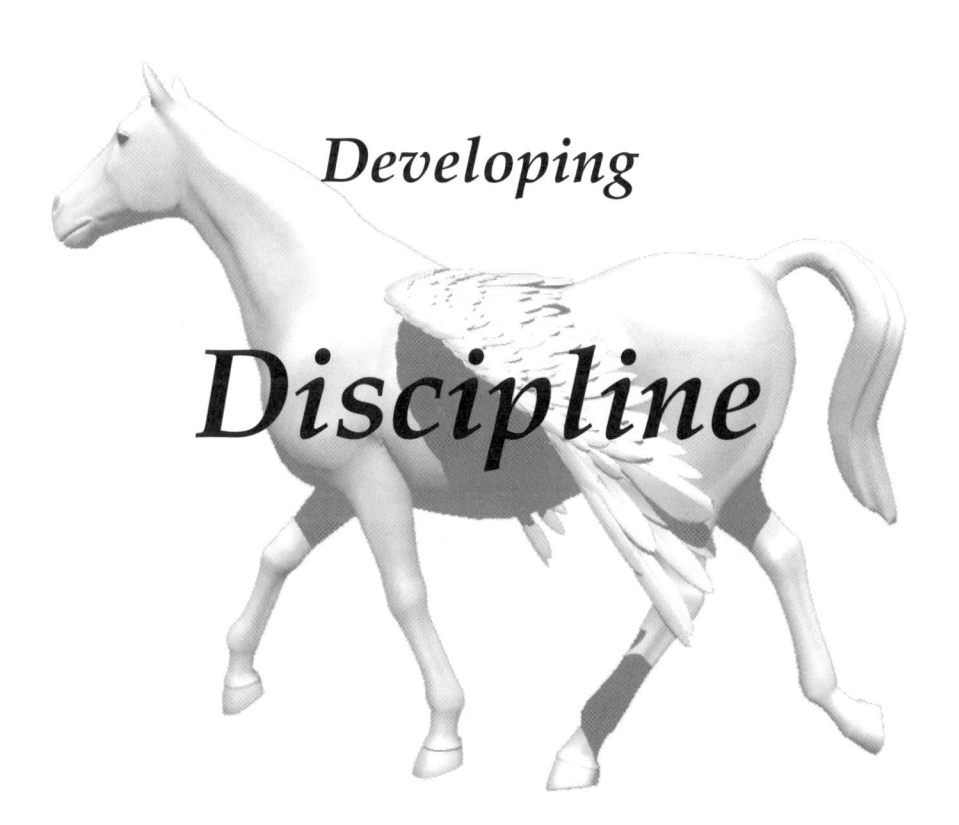

Discipline

Elizabeth Scott

Discipline *means self-control. Discipline can be divine in the miraculous results it produces. It can also be a curse if we move past discipline into rigidity that stifles our soul. Don't fear discipline, for it rarely turns to rigidity. Most of us err on the opposite end with our lax, procrastinating ways. Discipline can be a true-blue friend. Techniques in the next few chapters provide a good foundation for self-control without losing flexibility. Take a close look at these ideas for your life. Embrace discipline where you can.*

-10-

PUT THE DREAM INTO ACTION
Acquire portable skills to take on the road —

We've come far enough in our personal evaluation to hopefully pique your curiosity so we can take it to the next level — applying discipline to the dream. Now is the time to think about the nuts and bolts of a work and travel life. It's time to assemble a new way of living, step by step.

There are many portable skills to acquire for managing a business from home or the road. Some of the skills you may already have. Which specific skills you will need depend on the type of business you choose.

While you still have your "day job," begin taking classes in useful, portable skills. Consider whether you need a computer course to brush up on:

MOBILE COMPUTER SKILLS

Word processing	Bookkeeping
Tax accounting	Computer graphics
Databases	Internet research

When you buy software for these programs, they usually come with detailed instruction manuals. Some even have online tutorials. If not, bookstores often have independent manuals (like *Quicken for Dummies*). If you learn better in a classroom situation, sign up for night school, or check with your local computer store for classes. Allow plenty of time to complete necessary courses for your traveling business *before* you set up shop.

There are other less tangible skills you will want to acquire. At work, if someone else fixes the office machinery, start diving in and doing it yourself. Believe me, I hate interrupting my train of thought to straighten out an errant piece of machinery, but now is the time to learn the logic of these machines so you can fix them without help when you are on your own.

Check your local community college or high school for business classes in marketing, strategy, sales skills, negotiations and time management. Any business can be made better with effective sales, negotiations and marketing. And time management is crucial. Also check the business section in your bookstore or library for books on these subjects. There is a huge selection: Read the book jackets to determine which books will be most helpful to you. You can also go to the self-help or psychology section for books to boost your attitude if you are shy, negative, or lack focus.

Think of this learning phase as part of a self-test. You want to test your mettle in the discipline and dedication departments before you give up your current job. See what kind of self-starter you are. What kind of self-education program can you put together to fill the gaps in your business knowledge?

In your current work situation, what can you learn now that will help you segue into a "have work will travel" life? Take on everything that will elevate your credibility and level of competence. Your good reputation can pay off in referrals.

It's amazing how your present job experience can help you in a seemingly unrelated new career. For instance, I was able to apply the sales experience I gained in real estate and banking to my executive search work, which is so portable. Don't rule out a new industry where you can apply old skills.

And network, network, network! Many people think that

networking means being artificially nice to people in order to get something in return. This couldn't be further from the truth. Effective networking results from being thoughtful to every person you come in contact with, whether or not they are related to your job. It's not about a hidden agenda; it's about being nice.

As an example, I purchased some artwork from an artist named Susan and have referred several new clients to her. I like her as a person and have stayed in touch with her, even though we now live two states apart. Once, when my recruiting business was slow, she introduced me to a woman who became the largest single executive search client of my career. Buying artwork is not a traditional networking strategy, but this case was about becoming friends, without a hidden agenda. It became a networking coup by accident — if you believe in accidents.

You could also begin to take small steps toward having work that will travel. You might persuade your current boss to let you telecommute from home one day per week. Or work four long days and get three days off each week. Many employers are now more flexible about work schedules. Plan your case before presenting it.

Demonstrate how you will be effective and keep communication lines open. Emphasize that you will be more productive and explain why. For example, you will be able to use the time on work that you used to spend commuting, you will have fewer interruptions, or you will be available earlier (or later) than usual. Be sure to illustrate the benefits to the company. If your boss goes for it, you will have taken a major leap. If s/he is still hesitant, suggest a trial period — and then make sure you are productive and easy to reach so your manager will be willing to make the change permanent.

The plain truth is that you will always have a boss — even if you are an independent contractor, your customers are the boss.

They must have confidence in your dependability and competence, especially since you are not sitting where they can keep an eye on you.

And, no, I do not recommend pretending to be in town when you are traveling. The business world is accustomed to computers and cell phones. If you're doing a good job, most clients will not care where you are. Honesty is the best policy. For one thing, you will not be trusted if you are dishonest about your location and get caught. For another, it can actually be an icebreaker with a client. I have found many a cold-call phone conversation warmed up by banter about where I am working and traveling. People are naturally curious.

Whether you work for yourself or telecommute for an employer, cultivate the right client or boss relationship. If your current client/boss is opposed to work that will travel, you might need to get a new boss.

I watched Diana the Domestic Goddess do just that. She dumped her old boss and got into a productive and exciting job. Her new boss appreciates her so much that he allows her to take generous vacation time (probably six to eight weeks a year plus many long weekends). She's a good role model for all of us.

Diana was a happy homemaker: She stayed at home and raised her three children until they were grown. She and her husband traveled with the family a lot, and she loved their adventurous life. Once the children were older, she began working for a bank. Suddenly she had only two weeks of vacation per year and limited holidays. This was not what she bargained for.

She had a reputation among her friends for being supportive and helpful. She put the same cheery effort into every task at the bank, even though she was not thrilled with the vacation schedule. At work she continued her role as "Mom," taking care of everything at the office. And it paid off.

One of her acquaintances was a busy executive who needed a right-hand assistant to manage details for him. He knew that Diana the Domestic Goddess, with her upbeat efficiency, would be perfect. He recruited Diana away from the bank with a promise of more vacation time. She left the bank and became his executive secretary. She is indispensable to him, and he is happy to give her the travel time she craves.

Several important factors came into play here. One was that Diana was very well networked. She is friendly, outgoing and helpful. As a result of those qualities, she knows many people and makes a favorable impression. That led to the job with a great fit for travel.

Also notice that Diana carved a "have work will travel" life without going out on the self-employment limb. She did it with a safety net — working for someone who appreciates her and is flexible. She didn't miss a paycheck during the entire transition.

Listed below are a few examples of work that lends itself to travel. Some would allow you to work flexibly for an employer; others are more conducive to running your own business. Use these ideas to fuel your imagination:

WORK THAT FITS WITH TRAVEL

Computer graphics	Secretarial service
Billing service including phone collections	Phone sales
Executive recruiting	Journalism
Bookkeeping	Research
Real estate investment	Mail marketing
Event planning	Sewing or tailoring
Consulting in your previous line of work	Court reporter
Catering	Mortgage lending
Import/export	Airlines employment

You might even try something you haven't done before; discard it if it's a misfit and move on to a fresh choice, based on what you learned the first time. I certainly did a lot of trial and error, juggling several jobs at once to get the right balance of work, travel and income. I'll say it again, it takes dedication. If you don't succeed right away, stick with it and be flexible. Be willing to work hard to make your dream come true.

It is amazing how varied working-traveling careers can be. Remember my friend Judy Judge who travels with her husband Reggie Real Estate? We think of a judge as sitting in court all day, wearing a long black robe, and pounding a gavel. Yet Judy has been an active traveler for much of her legal career. Judges have to do a lot of research for each court case they hear. She is in town for court but has organized the research and opinion work so it can be done from anywhere.

One thing Judy Judge has done, which is important, is establish a strong home base. She travels a lot, but there is an office in her hometown with her main records and office equipment. She is there often enough to feel grounded.

It's a common mistake, once you have work that will travel, to be gone so much that you feel scattered and disoriented — this is NOT a productive way to work. So, like Judy Judge, establish a strong home base from which to operate, and be there enough to maintain a sense of stability. If you want a work-travel life for the long haul, don't burn yourself out with too much travel in too little time. Pace yourself so you can hold on to your dream.

-11-

ROLL UP YOUR SLEEVES
It's time to get started. Phones, computers, mail box service — Which tools are essential and when —

If you are ready to deal with the nuts and bolts of setting up your business, remember to **start simple.** Begin with your at-home workspace. Once you have that together, the mobile setup will naturally follow. Create your home environment before you give up your day job, so you have plenty of time to work out the kinks.

Begin shopping for equipment and services far in advance. Talk to people whose technical expertise you respect. Once you set up phone numbers, e-mail addresses and such, you will not want to make changes when your business is up and running. Changes are expensive: You must reprint office stationery and business cards, contact customers and affiliates with your revised information, and you may lose business if someone tries to reach you at your old numbers. It's better to get it right the first time, and if possible give your equipment and services a good long test-run.

There are basic tools of the trade necessary for almost any mobile business. Reduce your initial investment by using existing home equipment. Or buy used equipment from someone you know who is upgrading. Shop the discount stores and sales. Check out eBay and other auction sites for fantastic deals. Or even buy cheap equipment at first — you can upgrade later. After you upgrade, use the cheap stuff as portable equipment or in a secondary travel office (like a vacation home). Begin shopping and planning far in advance so you can thoroughly research quality and prices. Seize the moment when you find a great value.

Go to the library and look up the equipment you need in *Consumer Reports* magazine. You may want to subscribe to the magazine if you will be buying a lot of equipment over time. Their independent product reviews cover price, durability, cost to run, and performance. Their rating system is easy to understand, and they get no advertising revenue, so they are impartial.

There will be areas where you cannot afford to skimp, depending on the kind of business you start. For instance, a graphics business needs high-end computer and printing equipment, and expensive software. But if you are going to be successful in that line of work, you must know what you need, and what it costs. You can save by waiting for sales, using auction sites, and monitoring discount store inventories.

Almost every business will need these basics:

ESSENTIAL TOOLS OF THE TRADE

- Telephone. You will need to decide if you need more than one line. Do you need a cordless phone? A lot of speed-dial numbers? What about a built-in answering machine or caller ID? Think through the features you will need before you start shopping.

- Answering System. Voice mail has a monthly fee; an answering machine is a small one-time cost. Voice mail is more flexible — taking messages even if you are on the line or the electricity goes out. It can also include call waiting. However, you cannot screen calls with voice mail, like you can with an answering machine. Weigh your options and costs ahead of time.

- Second Phone Line. Most businesses need a dedicated line for faxes and/or the Internet. Even in less bureaucratic commerce like art and cooking, you must send bids, communications and invoices. A second line with no added options like call waiting or call forwarding can be inexpensive. There are usually installation charges, but it's often worth the investment.

- Cell Phone. When you begin traveling, you will want a good cell phone and cellular service. Research carefully and buy only a highly rated phone: It will make a huge difference in how long your battery lasts between charges, how well you hear others, how well others hear you, and how many dropped calls you suffer. The same care is needed to select a cellular service. Talk to people who are always on their cell phones. You know – the obnoxious ones who always have a cell phone to their ear while driving or eating, and even interrupt conversations to answer. They know which services are best in your area.

- Computer. Luckily prices are coming down. Depending on your need, you can spend well under $1,000 for a desktop. Laptops run a little more and tend to have less storage space and speed for the price. However, if you will be taking your computer with you in your work-travel life, you'll want to invest in a laptop from the beginning. I can do everything from my laptop and don't need a desktop computer for the home-based portion of my business. When I am at home, I attach a larger keyboard and mouse to my laptop and I can type at lightning speed (yeah, right).

- Fax. If you have a good fax program on your computer, you might not need a separate fax machine. I installed WinFaxPro on my computer and it does a better job than the program that came with the computer. But if you need to fax handwritten work, a computer fax will be insufficient, unless you want to invest in a scanner. Plain paper fax machines start well under $100. Make sure you buy all the features you need for your particular business.

You should also look into the multi-function machines for your home office. Their performance has improved greatly over the last few years while prices have shrunk to affordable levels. Better quality for less money, what a concept!

I have had good luck with a multi-function machine that cost about $450. It is a printer (photo quality), scanner, fax and copy machine. The print quality is high, and the machine is reliable and easy to use. I have a second machine that cost around $100 and performs the same functions (except scanning), in a vacation home. The print quality is much lower, and the machine seems to have more hiccups, but for my needs in a second home it is fine.

More thoughts on phone services: Should you get call forwarding? There is usually an extra fee for this service, but it can give a seamless appearance to clients by forwarding calls to your cell phone. Even better, I like "call following" which can be managed remotely. With call following, you can be off-site and set up your calls to forward to you, or change the destination number for forwarded calls, or discontinue forwarding — all without being anywhere near your main phone. Quite handy. Remember, if you forward calls to a long distance number, you will pay long distance fees for all your forwarded calls.

Call waiting is another add-on feature that I think is well worth the couple of dollars a month. It can be a less expensive alternative to installing a second phone line. When you are on the phone, call waiting notifies you when another call comes in. Call waiting combined with voice mail allows you to decide whether to interrupt your current call for another — if you do not take the second call, it will go into voice mail.

I wouldn't dream of working without my cordless phone and headset. I clip the phone on my belt or pocket and can take a call, walk to a file, or even into another room, without interrupting my conversation. And the little headset saves my neck! Before I got the headset, my neck always hurt because I tilted my head to hold the phone and free my hands to write or flip through papers. I was a regular at the chiropractor's office until I got the headset.

A 900 MHz (megahertz) cordless phone provides a reasonable walking distance from the phone base. Including a headset, a name brand phone can be found for $20 or less, if you shop carefully. I have one set for each line in my home office, plus a travel set. They are so compact that they easily fit into a suitcase for a trip. When I arrive, I plug my cordless phone into the "auxiliary" jack on the land phone in my room.

The only downside with the clip-on phone and headset is that if I get carried away and move around too much, the clip slips off my belt and the phone drops to the floor. Or I move up against a desk, bump the phone, and disconnect the call. Occasionally, the other party has difficulty hearing me through the headset; however, when I stick to highly rated phones, the weak connection is a rare occurrence.

Your choice of long distance carrier is also an important one, so shop carefully. If you are paying more than 6 cents per minute, you can do better, including unlimited minutes around the clock. Some companies even throw in a calling card for the same per-minute rate with no additional fees. Calling cards are handy on the road when a cell phone is not an option. Check with friends, and run a search on the Internet for "long distance carriers." On my most recent search, I found a plan for 4.5 cents per minute. It took me less than a minute to gather all the information I needed. I have yet to find a major phone service provider whose long distance rates are better than independent competitors, and the competitors make the changeover easy.

When you shop, look beyond the cents per minute they quote. Ask if they "prorate the minutes." This means if your call lasts 5 1/2 minutes, they charge for 5 1/2 minutes. Many

companies charge more by "rounding up" to 6 minutes. This adds up over the course of a month. With a service that rounds up to the next minute your phone bill might look something like this:
1. GA&G Phone Company charges 4.5 cents per minute.
2. You use 750 minutes talking long distance in January (12 1/2 hours).
3. The phone company rounds up to the next highest minute each time you hang up the phone.
4. They bill you for **938** minutes because of the rounding up.
5. Your bill for long distance is:

        4.5 cents per minute
    x   938 minutes billed
    $ 42.21 for January's long distance

Had you signed up instead with SMAR&T Phone Company who rounds up in 6-second intervals your bill would look like this:
1. SMAR&T also charges 4.5 cents per minute.
2. They round up to the next tenth of a minute each time you hang up the phone (6 seconds).
3. You talk for 750 minutes in January.
4. They bill you for 768.8 minutes.
5. Your long distance bill is:

        4.5 cents per minute
    x   768.8 minutes billed
    $ 34.60 for January

You save $7.41 per month or $88.92 per year if you go with SMAR&T. While we are not talking the National Debt here, why let GA&G Phone Company have that money? It adds up to almost $90 a year that you could use yourself. You could take your savings to a discount store and buy a cordless phone and headset for your office, *plus* a cordless phone and headset for your travels, plus a compact answering machine for travel — all for only $90.

Calling cards: If your new long distance carrier does not provide a calling card, you can buy one at all kinds of stores – from supermarkets to gas stations. One of the best prices I've found was at a discount warehouse — only $20 for many hours of carefree talking.

The downside to calling cards is that they are cumbersome to use. It is a laborious process to place a series of calls using a calling card: You have to enter a long stream of numbers before you can even begin to dial the phone number you'd like to reach. To get around this, set up your calling card numbers to speed-dial on the phone you use the most. It will ease your frustration and minimize the calluses on your dialing finger.

Calling cards are a bargain almost anywhere *except* cruise ships — ship-to-shore calls cost an arm and a leg. The Internet is the most cost-effective way to communicate from a cruise ship, unless you can send Morse Code signals! Cruise ships often have libraries with comfortable view rooms housing computers with free Internet access.

Cell phone information: The cell phone will be your most useful tool when you travel. You can forward all your business and personal calls so you never need to call home for messages. If you have call forwarding, there is no need to give out your cell number — those who call your business line will be forwarded to you automatically. With a cell phone you can be easily reached while traveling, and you can turn the ringer off when you want to take a break.

After you choose a highly rated cell phone, shop just as carefully for your service provider. If you know you will often be in particular rural areas, check the provider's service area map to be sure you will have service there. Some cellular services even provide reciprocal phone service with competitors — when you are outside your provider's area, the competitor's service handles your calls. If the map looks dismal, see what kind of reciprocal arrangements they provide. Those reciprocal agreements can eliminate expensive roaming charges.

When you set up your cell phone and service, make sure it has a voice mail feature. This is crucial. Cellular voice mail will usually take messages for you even when you are out of cell range; you are never completely out of touch.

Set up your cellular outgoing message with the same greeting as your home office greeting. Then the system is truly seamless. Callers can't tell whether you are in your office or on the road if your message sounds the same.

Cell phones are usually very expensive to use from foreign countries. This is where the long distance calling card you have shopped for so carefully will come in handy. While cell phone calls might cost several dollars per minute, a good calling card could be under one dollar per minute from a foreign country. If you travel out of the country often, and need to be in phone contact, do your research carefully to get good rates.

Computer highlights: I am anything but a computer nerd. So I'll keep it simple.

A laptop is almost essential to work that travels. One way around the laptop issue when you travel is to rent computer time in cybercafés and office centers like Kinko's. Or go to a well-equipped computer store and rent a computer. It's even cheaper to find a library with computers and use one for free. You can carry disks with the work you need. However, if your work requires special software or access to elaborate databases, borrowing a computer will not do the job. Then you will need a portable laptop with the software and data installed.

Copy machine, to buy or not to buy: If your copy needs are infrequent, the local print shop will suffice. Also a simple fax machine can copy most documents. Only if your business is heavy in paperwork, like mortgage lending, will you need to start off with a copy machine.

Peripheral equipment that will travel: There are portable computer printers on the market if you need to print a lot of material from the road. However, if you carry a laptop, cell phone, cordless phone, *and* portable printer, you probably won't fit your luggage in the overhead bin on an airplane. Portable printers are great for longer trips where you will settle into one place. In a pinch, when I have no printer, I fax pages from my computer's fax program to a local fax machine. There are fax notations on the top of the page, so this solution works only when the output does not need to be perfectly clean.

You can also copy your work onto a disk and take it to a nearby copy center, computer store, or other business, and rent a computer to print your work.

Avoid fax machines that use rolled fax paper. The print quality is usually poor. The paper comes out curled, and is a strange, thin texture. The faxed copies also tend to fade quickly. With plain paper fax machines costing so little now, there is no monetary incentive to put up with the inconvenience of paper rolls.

Portable peripheral equipment should be a secondary investment — after your traveling business is well on the road. There are short-term ways to get around the need for portable printers, fax machines and so forth. If "have work will travel" becomes a long-term lifestyle, and the portable equipment will make a big difference, then go ahead and make the investment. Until then, the laptop and cell phone will address most working needs while traveling.

Personal organizers, pro and con: I happen to like keeping all my basic data in one place. My mind gets scattered when I have little pieces of paper all over the place. Those little Post-Its tend to get lost, along with my thoughts. Some people like reminder notes here, there and everywhere, but I just can't do it. I need a single organizer with my calendar, shopping lists, birthdays, addresses and phone numbers. If it takes up more than three by five inches, I don't want it in my purse. This makes small electronic daytimers great for me.

More linear thinkers do better seeing a week-at-a-glance. If they can see what was yesterday and what will be tomorrow, everything comes into focus. For such a thinker, written daytimers keep their mind less cluttered and the added bulk of a week-at-a-glance or day-at-a-glance organizer is worth it to them.

Many people like personal data assistants (PDAs) such as Visors and Palm Pilots, but they are expensive if you are watching your start-up costs. They are great for organizing data and keeping up with e-mail. However, a PDA usually won't eliminate the need for a computer. I consider them luxuries, not necessities.

Whether you prefer an electronic or paper system, anyone who is working and traveling needs an organizational tool. You must be at peak efficiency as you add travel to your work. Be sure to become accustomed to using your organizing system before you hit the road, so it's second nature to you.

Mail box rental services: A mail box rental service, like Mail Boxes Etc., pays for itself in many ways: For about $10 per month, you get a mailing address, a mail box, a key, and often 24-hour access. This gives you privacy if you need it. Your mail box address can be printed on stationery and business cards, rather than your home address. Price will vary depending on location, though. Urban areas tend to charge more.

In addition you get short-term mail forwarding service that a U.S. Postal facility will not provide. If you will be traveling for two weeks or more, mail forwarding is a must. There is usually a nominal fee for handling (*i.e.*, $3.50), plus the postage expense. With forwarding, your bills and other important mail are never too far behind, and you are spared the chore of notifying others of your temporary address.

Set up your mail box service early in your business setup, so you can print business cards, stationery and other items with the right address from the beginning.

Even my friend Annabelle Artiste has done well setting up her "have work will travel" business. She claims to have no business sense at all, yet she stays organized and in touch when she travels with her work. She uses her artistic skills professionally as a jewelry designer. She travels to department stores in major cities and markets her line of jewelry. She also travels to purchase semi-precious stones and other materials for her creations.

So how does an "artiste" use office equipment in her business and personal travel life? The answer is, very effectively. Annabelle's computer use is less involved than that of many business people, so she goes to a nearby Kinko's business center and rents computer time for her word processing and Internet needs. Her faxes come and go through Kinko's as well. She does not need to carry a laptop computer.

Annabelle is always near her cell phone, and doesn't miss client calls while she works around the nation. Her home number forwards to her cell phone so clients need only one phone number to reach her.

Ms. Artiste loves to joke about how electronically challenged she is; she does not use an electronic organizer for her scheduling and phone numbers. She keeps them in an attractive clothbound book that appeals to her sense of aesthetics.

Even though she is often gone for a week or two at a time, she has not set up a mail box service. Her husband forwards anything important or reads it to her over the phone. That is a money-saver for Annabelle.

By paying to use a print shop's computer and fax, and using a family member's help to keep up with "snail" mail, Annabelle Artiste's travel equipment is minimal. She travels light and keeps her business head about her with just her cell phone.

-12-

TAKE IT ON THE ROAD
Juggle transportation, lodging, and keep up the work flow —

There are many settings in which you may work when you travel — a hotel, motel, family or friend's home, or an office in another city. How you organize your work space will vary as widely as where you set up shop, but there are some common elements no matter where you stay.

Think ahead so you can create a quiet place to work, yet be considerate of others with whom you share the space. You must often share phone lines and other vital work resources, as well as the kitchen, laundry, bedroom, bathroom and other personal resources. Rules of etiquette help to keep everyone happy and you, productive. Each form of lodging has its own nuances.

Hotel or motel

If you share a hotel room, lay the ground rules before you start work. Ask for quiet time during the work hours you want. Usually, if you ask ahead of time, roommates are happy to oblige. The courtesy of a request, instead of a demand, encourages cooperation. And, if you give the other person advance notice, they can plan their activities accordingly.

If a roomie knows you'll be on the phone and computer from 10 in the morning until noon, and from three to five in the afternoon, he or she can plan to be up and out the door, having breakfast and enjoying the day, as you get started. If you wait until the last minute to explain your schedule, s/he may plan to sleep in or return in the late afternoon, smack dab in the middle of your work. Asking ahead of time also allows a roomie to plan when s/he can make phone calls, so that resentment doesn't build up.

If your roommate objects to the work hours you request, find out why. Respectfully negotiate a compromise that will allow you to get your job done, and allow your roomie to access the room when needed. Be very careful to keep the peace. It will make the trip a lot more fun for everyone, and you'll get more concessions when you need them.

Travel with a companion usually means sharing equipment and services. Coordinate this with your travel mate in advance. Think through solutions before you have problems. If you are both actively working while you travel, you will each need your own laptop and cell phone. You could also, in advance, locate an office center, library or other place to access a computer and phone, and have quiet time.

Most hotels have a phone with an auxiliary jack for plugging in your laptop to the Internet. The phones will often include voice mail (with a generic outgoing message). Some hotels provide fax service at the front desk for a per-page fee. Or they can often recommend nearby facilities for additional business needs you may have. Call your hotel in advance to see what services they offer the business traveler.

Motels have lower prices and streamlined services: You can't count on an auxiliary phone jack, fax service or recommendations for business facilities. You can log onto the Internet ahead of time, however, and search the Yellow Pages for computer rentals and copy centers.

Friend or family home

Cooperation is often easier in a private home setting because there are more rooms available for everyone. Of course, there are also often more people to distract you from your work. Tell everyone ahead of time that if you close the door to your work area, you don't mean to be rude; you are just letting people know you are working and need a little quiet. If you say this in advance, you'll be more comfortable isolating yourself for work, and your friends will be less likely to take offense.

If you are in someone's home and they are present, be very careful not to monopolize their phone. Even if they say, "Oh, go ahead! It won't bother me," tread very carefully. It is still *their* phone, as it is *their* house. Put yourself in your host's place. Pack your cell phone. When you must use their phone line for the Internet, ask each time before you log on. And do your online work as quickly as possible, so you don't overextend your welcome to the phone line.

There can be a lot of fun comings-and-goings in a household where you are a guest. Maintain discipline. Promise yourself and your friends a certain amount of time to play. Both you and your hosts will feel less deprived. Use the **Two-Hour Rule** and the **Two-Day Rule.** Every workday that you travel, set aside two hours to go sightseeing, hike, shop, visit friends or do whatever is fun where you are visiting. Just a quick getaway, then back to work. And be more generous with your days off while traveling. I try to take off three or four days a week when I travel. That leaves me enough time to be productive, but still get out and adventure. As a bare minimum, take two days off each week to enjoy your destination.

If responsibilities keep you from taking more than two days off in a given week, don't resent it. Stick doggedly to the Two-Hour Rule. Take off two extra hours each day to do something exciting, then get back to business. By maximizing your weekend time (or whatever days you usually take off), you'll get out more and enjoy the places you travel.

Office in another city

If you travel and are lucky enough to have access to a friend's or associate's office, seize the opportunity. It will solve most of your logistical problems. There are usually adequate phone lines, office equipment and space. While the environment is usually productive, tread lightly, just like in a host's home. Don't spread out and encroach on other people's space or monopolize their phones and equipment. Ask permission for everything. You are still on someone else's turf.

Bring your own laptop when using someone else's office. It's hard to use someone else's computer, since you won't be familiar with the software. Also, if you inadvertently damage their files or crash their computer, you probably won't be invited back.

You may be able to download their printer's software to your laptop and use the printer at your host-office. But don't park your computer on their printer for the entire stay. Just hook up when you need to print, and then reconnect the printer the way it was: ready for your host to use.

If you cannot hook up to their printer, and you have fax software on your computer, send your document to their fax machine for a hard copy — just keep in mind it will have fax notations at the top of the pages. And there must be a dedicated fax line so you don't get a busy signal when you fax from in-house.

More rustic environments

If your travels are more down to earth, staying in youth hostels or camping, you probably won't be able to place and receive business calls from your place of lodging. A cell phone is an option if you are within range of cellular service. If cellular service is not available, don't despair. There is a way out, but it takes some planning and will be inconvenient.

Research your trip carefully and camp or lodge near a town that has a business center, computer store, print shop or other venue with the office equipment you'll need. Given the difficulty of these logistics, minimize the amount of time you spend working. Limit it to checking phone messages and e-mail, and handling any urgent matters.

Jake the Jock, a real estate investor, uses this limited form of "have work will travel." He travels a lot, and while on the road, keeps up with phone messages and "puts out fires." However, he doesn't keep up with e-mail or deal with complex paperwork. He spends his travel days hiking, cycling, at the gym, and participating in a variety of outdoor sports.

Jake leads a fast-paced life and has admirable discipline as he mixes work and play. He says he's too busy to figure out how to do mobile computing or get his bills forwarded to him while he travels. He doesn't want to be bothered. Sometimes details slip through the cracks while he is away.

Jake is fairly happy with this arrangement, though he is not happy when he returns to overwhelming stacks of mail and tasks that have piled up. While he has work that will travel, it could use a little fine-tuning. If Jake made a short list of his strengths and weaknesses, he might find a solution to his dilemma.

STRENGTHS	WEAKNESSES
Disciplined	Impatient
Adventurous	Refuses to read instruction manuals
Creative problem-solver	Overlooks details
Successful in business	Computer semiliterate

These are the traits that directly affect Jake's work-travel limitations. He just needs to fine-tune his road show. The fact that he is already **successful in business** while traveling means that he has some great resources. Using his **creative problem-solving** ability, he can conquer his **computer semiliteracy** and handle more tasks on the road.

Jake has the financial resources to hire an assistant. An assistant could help with computer tasks and see that business details get attention and perhaps teach Jake enough computer skills to make him more efficient on the road.

The new approach might look something like this: Jake works with his assistant about five hours a week when he is at home. The assistant does filing, simple phone tasks, maintains databases, and gives Jake a half-hour computer lesson each week. A brief lesson would get around Jake's **impatience.** The lessons would cover e-mail and portable computer options.

Jake's new assistant could help him learn to use a financial program, like Quicken, which would allow Jake to pay bills from the road. Many banks offer electronic banking through the Internet. While Jake might not have the patience to set it up, his assistant certainly would. Once the Internet bill-pay system is in place, and Jake knows how to use it at home, he can take it on the road. And he would be computer savvy, instead of **computer semiliterate.**

Internet banking services usually cost $6 or $7 per month. However, since they reduce the cost of printed checks and postage for mailing bills, the net expense is negligible. The service is fast and easy to use. Jake can pay the newspaper boy and the gardener via the Internet, as well as his utilities and charge cards. He can use a tickler system in the Internet banking calendar or in his financial program to remind him when bills are due while he travels. No checkbook to carry. No bills to truck around — just a disk to back up his work.

If Jake doesn't have the patience to use the electronic tickler system, his assistant can create a computer database of Jake's "Bills to Pay" and print it out. Taking this one-page document with him on the road, Jake will know when each bill is due. An example of this document is on the next page. Every list of "Bills to Pay" should include: date to pay, date due, company name, account number, phone number, address and payment amount. You'll find a blank form on page 122, as well as in Addendum IV, that you can photocopy and complete with your own schedule of bills.

To avoid frustration, Jake's assistant could walk him through computer tasks by phone if he gets stuck. Jake could pay for this service in quarter-hour increments. His assistant could also pick up his mail about twice a week and let Jake know, from return addresses, what has come in. If something is urgent, s/he can forward it to him.

Jake the Jock's situation is a case of taking a good thing and making it better. Jake could have a happier return home if he kept up with his computer work and bills from the road. Plus, when Jake is home, he'd have an assistant to handle pesky details, since Jake the Jock is so **disinterested in details.**

BILLS TO PAY

PAY	DUE	COMPANY	ACCOUNT #	PHONE #	ADDRESS	AMOUNT
10th	18th	Gage Gas & Elect.	5423-198-00X	800-234-0111	PO Box 7658, LA, CA 90000	call for quote
10th	20th	Cable TV	SO7-3258-69	888-118-3106	PO Box 51000, LA, CA 90001	$58.68
10th	25th	Zippy Cellular Svc	528-630-5111 NZ	611	3111 5th Ave, Pinecrest, CA 90012	$89.99
18th	30th	Ding Dong Bell	528-924-8830 SNR	800-ASK BELL	PO Box 311, LA, CA 90009	call for quote
18th	18th	Western Bank	059-300510-7	888 THE BANK	Internet banking pmt, auto trans.	$6.95
18th	18th	ABC Internet Service	my e-mail address	877-377-2940	Auto transfer	$19.95
18th	1st	Ace Water	559-32-8885	310-888-5500	PO Box 31950, LA, CA 90049	call for quote
18th	1st	Bank Platinum Card	9131-6789560-5678	88PLATINUM	PO Box 1, LA, CA 90031	$200
1st	15th	Big Bank, mortgage	654-897-0001	310-854-8976	PO Box 25377, LA, CA 90003	$2450.79
1st	15th	Smaller S&L Loan	SVX-300-AVX-9	888-456-7890	PO Box 57911, LA, CA 90008	$5490.63

QUARTERLY, SEMI-ANNUAL AND ANNUAL PAYMENTS

PAY	DUE	COMPANY	ACCOUNT #	PHONE #	ADDRESS	AMOUNT
Mar 15	Mar 29	Safety Insurance, Hse	VIN-30-5610	888-1SAFETY	PO Box 90012, Scottsbluff, NE 69300	$779.31
May 15	May 26	BBB Auto Club	883-9936579-ES	888-BBB-BEST	PO Box 4500, Phoenix, AZ 85039	$79.00
Sept 15	Sept 2	Safety Insurance, Hse	EOS-30-5610	888-1SAFETY	PO Box 90012, Scottsbluff, NE 69300	$779.31
Nov 26	Dec 15	Safety Insurance, Car	VIN-45-0001	888-1SAFETY	PO Box 90011, Scottsbluff, NE 69300	$2930.10

Elizabeth Scott

BILLS TO PAY

PAY	DUE	COMPANY	ACCOUNT #	PHONE #	ADDRESS	AMOUNT

QUARTERLY, SEMI-ANNUAL AND ANNUAL PAYMENTS

-13-

NUTS, BOLTS AND TOOLBOXES
*Transport all the tools of the trade **and** the toys —*

The first few times you try to work and travel, you may wonder if the lifestyle is really worth all the planning and coordination it requires. But after a few trial runs, you'll begin to refine the process and simplify every step. Then it will start to seem worthwhile. So, hang in there! It gets easier with every trip you take.

Through trial and error, you will determine which tools you really need on the road and which ones you can do without. Traveling light is much easier than being bogged down with a ton of luggage. So gradually pare down to the essentials. I call these essentials my "nuts and bolts."

Something that has simplified my life tremendously is a travel list. It starts with a little to-do list to make sure I take care of last-minute chores before locking up the house. Then it lists the items I take with me for business and personal use. It also has a mini-list of sports equipment for summer and winter sports that I like. You'll find a copy of my "Travel List" on pages 125-126. It has a row of check boxes next to each item so I can use the same list many times.

I do not take every item on the list on every trip. Some are for road trips; others are for plane trips and cruises. Everything is on one list, in one place, so I won't forget anything when it is needed.

You can copy this list for your use. There are spaces for you to add items if need be. Or use the "Travel List" as a model to create your own list if your travel needs vary drastically from mine. You can find a copy of this list in Addendum V. Also compare this "Travel List" to the "World Traveler's Packing List" on pages 127-129 and Addendum VI. It is a generic travel list I found in my Microsoft Works program.

The main thing is to find a simple way to list your regular travel items. It makes packing go much faster and you are far less likely to forget something important.

Have Work Will Travel

TRAVEL LIST

Travel keys	❏❏❏❏❏❏	Turn off computer	❏❏❏❏❏❏
Airline ticket	❏❏❏❏❏❏	Set call following	❏❏❏❏❏❏
Itinerary	❏❏❏❏❏❏	Drapes closed	❏❏❏❏❏❏
Passport	❏❏❏❏❏❏	Set light timers	❏❏❏❏❏❏
Maps	❏❏❏❏❏❏	Heater off	❏❏❏❏❏❏
Cash, traveler's checks	❏❏❏❏❏❏	Garbage out	❏❏❏❏❏❏
		Water plants	❏❏❏❏❏❏
Daytimer	❏❏❏❏❏❏	Discard old food	❏❏❏❏❏❏
Cell phone	❏❏❏❏❏❏	Give travel #s to family	❏❏❏❏❏❏
Headset	❏❏❏❏❏❏		
Cell AC charger	❏❏❏❏❏❏		
Cell auto charger	❏❏❏❏❏❏	Casual clothes	❏❏❏❏❏❏
Laptop computer	❏❏❏❏❏❏	Business clothes	❏❏❏❏❏❏
Computer charger	❏❏❏❏❏❏	Lingerie	❏❏❏❏❏❏
Floppy disks/CDs	❏❏❏❏❏❏	Nylons	❏❏❏❏❏❏
Project files	❏❏❏❏❏❏	Underwear	❏❏❏❏❏❏
Pen, pencil, marker	❏❏❏❏❏❏	Socks	❏❏❏❏❏❏
Computer paper	❏❏❏❏❏❏	Nightgown, robe	❏❏❏❏❏❏
Answering machine	❏❏❏❏❏❏	Slippers	❏❏❏❏❏❏
Cordless phone	❏❏❏❏❏❏		
Headset	❏❏❏❏❏❏		
Fax/phone cords	❏❏❏❏❏❏	Umbrella	❏❏❏❏❏❏
Phone 2-in-1 adapter	❏❏❏❏❏❏	Gloves	❏❏❏❏❏❏
Phone cord coupler	❏❏❏❏❏❏	Hair clips	❏❏❏❏❏❏
Checkbook	❏❏❏❏❏❏	Day pack	❏❏❏❏❏❏
Calculator	❏❏❏❏❏❏	Gym clothes, shoes	❏❏❏❏❏❏
Apron	❏❏❏❏❏❏		
Recipes	❏❏❏❏❏❏		
Food bars	❏❏❏❏❏❏	Sunglasses	❏❏❏❏❏❏
Cosmetics case	❏❏❏❏❏❏	Swimsuit, goggles	❏❏❏❏❏❏
Prescriptions	❏❏❏❏❏❏	Sunscreen	❏❏❏❏❏❏
Vitamins	❏❏❏❏❏❏	Shaver	❏❏❏❏❏❏
Herbal supplements	❏❏❏❏❏❏		
Tums, eye drops	❏❏❏❏❏❏	Hair dryer	❏❏❏❏❏❏
		Fingernail polish	❏❏❏❏❏❏
		Polish remover pads	❏❏❏❏❏❏
Music CDs, tapes	❏❏❏❏❏❏		
Books, magazines	❏❏❏❏❏❏		
Camera, film	❏❏❏❏❏❏		
Notepad	❏❏❏❏❏❏		

Elizabeth Scott

SKIING:
Goggles ❏ ❏ ❏ ❏ ❏ ❏
Hat, muffler ❏ ❏ ❏ ❏ ❏ ❏
Gloves, liners ❏ ❏ ❏ ❏ ❏ ❏
Skis, poles ❏ ❏ ❏ ❏ ❏ ❏
Boots ❏ ❏ ❏ ❏ ❏ ❏
After ski boots ❏ ❏ ❏ ❏ ❏ ❏
Ski clothes ❏ ❏ ❏ ❏ ❏ ❏

HIKING:
Boots ❏ ❏ ❏ ❏ ❏ ❏
Sock liners ❏ ❏ ❏ ❏ ❏ ❏
Hiking socks ❏ ❏ ❏ ❏ ❏ ❏
Hiking pants ❏ ❏ ❏ ❏ ❏ ❏
Fleece jacket ❏ ❏ ❏ ❏ ❏ ❏
Water purification kit ❏ ❏ ❏ ❏ ❏ ❏
Water bottle ❏ ❏ ❏ ❏ ❏ ❏

SUMMER:
Visor ❏ ❏ ❏ ❏ ❏ ❏
Sun hat ❏ ❏ ❏ ❏ ❏ ❏
Snorkel equipment ❏ ❏ ❏ ❏ ❏ ❏

BICYCLING:
Helmet ❏ ❏ ❏ ❏ ❏ ❏
Cycling pants, top ❏ ❏ ❏ ❏ ❏ ❏
Windbreaker ❏ ❏ ❏ ❏ ❏ ❏

MOTORCYCLE:
Helmet ❏ ❏ ❏ ❏ ❏ ❏
Goggles ❏ ❏ ❏ ❏ ❏ ❏
Jacket ❏ ❏ ❏ ❏ ❏ ❏
Boots ❏ ❏ ❏ ❏ ❏ ❏
Rain gear ❏ ❏ ❏ ❏ ❏ ❏

World Traveler's Packing List

THE BASICS

- ❑ Cargo bag/suitcase
- ❑ Shoulder bag/daypack
- ❑ Luggage ID tags
- ❑ Personal/student ID & driver's license
- ❑ Wallet and cash
- ❑ Traveler's checks
- ❑ Passport, visa, and tourist card
- ❑ Money belt and passport carrier
- ❑ Tickets
- ❑ Credit and telephone cards
- ❑ Health insurance card
- ❑ Emergency contact information
- ❑ Address book
- ❑ Phrase books and guide books
- ❑ Maps
- ❑ _____
- ❑ _____

CLOTHING

- ❑ Rain gear or seasonal coat
- ❑ Comfortable walking shoes
- ❑ Dress shoes
- ❑ Athletic shoes
- ❑ Sandals
- ❑ Rubber thongs/slaps
- ❑ Sweater
- ❑ Shirts/blouses
- ❑ T-shirts
- ❑ Jeans
- ❑ Slacks
- ❑ Shorts
- ❑ Underwear
- ❑ Socks
- ❑ Seasonal hat
- ❑ Gloves/mittens
- ❑ Bandanna
- ❑ Belt
- ❑ Long underwear
- ❑ Swimsuit
- ❑ Pajamas or nightgown
- ❑ Bathrobe and slippers
- ❑ _____
- ❑ _____

For Women

- ❑ Dress
- ❑ Skirt
- ❑ Slip
- ❑ Stockings/tights
- ❑ _____
- ❑ _____

For Men

- ❑ Tie
- ❑ Belt/suspenders
- ❑ Tuxedo
- ❑ _____
- ❑ _____

PERSONAL

- ❏ Soap and container
- ❏ Toilet paper
- ❏ Medicines and prescriptions
- ❏ Vitamins
- ❏ Shampoo
- ❏ Comb and brush
- ❏ Toothbrush, toothpaste, and floss
- ❏ Lip balm and sun screen
- ❏ Small towel and washcloth
- ❏ Premoistened towelettes
- ❏ Deodorant
- ❏ Earplugs
- ❏ Hairdryer
- ❏ Hair spray/mousse
- ❏ Saline solution
- ❏ Extra pair of glasses/contacts & prescription
- ❏ Sunglasses
- ❏ Feminine hygiene products
- ❏ Make up
- ❏ Razor and blades
- ❏ Shaving cream
- ❏ Aftershave
- ❏ _____
- ❏ _____

For Children and Infants

- ❏ Diapers and diaper wipes
- ❏ Toys and books
- ❏ Formula
- ❏ Bottles, brushes, and accessories
- ❏ Night light
- ❏ _____
- ❏ _____

OTHER USEFUL ITEMS

- ❏ Dried fruit & healthful snacks
- ❏ Books and magazines
- ❏ Playing cards
- ❏ Notebook and pen
- ❏ Stationery, envelopes, and stamps
- ❏ Business cards
- ❏ Inflatable pillow
- ❏ Emergency space blanket
- ❏ Pocket hammock
- ❏ Coat hangers
- ❏ Nylon cord/clothes line
- ❏ Laundry soap
- ❏ Flat rubber drain plug
- ❏ Scrub brush
- ❏ Voltage adapter and plug adapters
- ❏ Batteries
- ❏ Binoculars
- ❏ Sheet bag for hostels
- ❏ Small flashlight
- ❏ Watch and alarm clock
- ❏ Video camera, camera, & film
- ❏ Travel iron or steamer
- ❏ Sewing kit with safety pins
- ❏ Umbrella
- ❏ Compass
- ❏ Safety pins
- ❏ Sealable plastic bags
- ❏ Rip-stop repair tape
- ❏ Combination lock
- ❏ Nylon duffel (folded)
- ❏ Small nylon bags
- ❏ _____
- ❏ _____
- ❏ _____

CAMPING EQUIPMENT

❑ Sleeping bag and pad
❑ Tent
❑ Ground cloth
❑ Water bottle/canteen
❑ Cup
❑ Fork and spoon
❑ Cook kit
❑ Stove and fuel
❑ Matches
❑ Insect repellent
❑ Small first aid kit
❑ First aid booklet
❑ Blister kit
❑ Water purification tablets
❑ Water filter
❑ Pocket knife with tools
❑ Pocket sharpening stone
❑ Snake bite kit
❑ Hiking boots
❑ _____
❑ _____

ADDITIONAL TRAVEL GEAR

❑ Pet food and toys
❑ Laptop computer
❑ Portable printer and scanner
❑ _____
❑ _____
❑ _____
❑ _____
❑ _____
❑ _____
❑ _____

I have a small briefcase that fits in my travel bag. It is permanently packed with the following:

- Paper clips
- Small scissors (do *not* carry on a plane)
- Mini-stapler
- Phone & address database
- "Bills to Pay List" (pages 122 or 188)
- Business travel file
- Medical insurance information
- Floppy disks or blank CDs
- Travel calendar
- Stamps
- Envelopes and stationery
- Phone cords & line extenders
- Pen, pencil and marker
- Batteries for electronic gadgets

We will talk more about what to keep permanently packed and how to organize it in Chapter 14 and Addendum VII. With these "nuts and bolts" always packed to go, I don't clutter my mind with minutia before I travel. It's like a toolbox, ready at a moment's notice.

Personal items can be prepacked too. My cosmetics case unfolds and hangs on a door handle, so it doesn't take up bathroom counter space. It is permanently packed with the lotions and potions I need on the road. Notice my "Travel List" does not include shampoo, lotion, makeup, hairbrush or face cleanser. This is because they are always packed in my cosmetic case along with Band-Aids, cough drops, aspirin, deodorant, and a mini-sewing kit, like the kind you find in hotel hospitality trays. Just one item on the list, "cosmetic case," covers all those things. This cosmetic bag can do double duty at home — it goes into my gym bag when I work out.

Everything I travel with is in small containers that I refill as needed when I return from a trip (when what is needed is fresh in my mind). An alternative is to save hotel shampoos and lotions to replenish your travel kit.

Early in your travel life, I recommend that you invest in

these two compact "toolboxes" that fit inside your luggage. First purchase a lightweight briefcase to fill with business tools: A soft-sided nylon briefcase with a few compartments is perfect. Then buy a cosmetic case ("travel kit" for the guys) to carry lotions and potions. Each of these cases can be found in discount stores for under $20.

I have some favorite nuts and bolts to keep in the briefcase, which allow me to adapt to almost any phone situation I encounter on the road. I keep a small plastic bag with a few pieces of phone equipment. It takes up almost no space but is infinitely valuable to me. It includes two compactly bound phone cords: one is for a telephone and one for a computer. So I can use both phone cords with a single wall jack, I have a 2-in-1 adapter. I also pack a phone cord coupler — it allows me to combine the two medium-length phone cords into one long cord. These phone accessories can be found in many supermarkets, almost all hardware stores, discount superstores like OfficeMax, and at specialty stores like Radio Shack.

I have used at least one of these phone accessories on every work trip I have taken. The little nuts and bolts can make a big difference.

Keeping electronic gadgets secure and intact during rough-and-tumble travel can be a challenge. A carry-on suitcase with wheels is the best way to go, whether traveling by plane, train or car. Pack your laptop in a padded computer bag. Either carry the bag on your shoulder or fit it into your carry-on suitcase. Incidentals like cordless phones, headsets and answering machines can take a little more abuse and are cheaply replaced. They can be checked on a plane or packed in a larger bag with clothes. Wrap them in sweaters, socks, jeans and other clothing for padding. Tuck small items into shoes for pretty good protection.

If you have irreplaceable documents in your briefcase, put

it in your carry-on with the computer. If the papers are not critical, they can be left in your larger luggage and checked. I usually put my briefcase and computer bag into the carry-on (after removing scissors, letter openers and other airport security red flags). I have a second, soft-sided shoulder bag that holds jewelry, travel documents, purse, and essentials. Everything else gets packed into a larger bag that I check on the plane. I don't mind if baggage handlers and bellmen handle the big bag; however, I am the only one who picks up the carry-on containing my electronics and business information. This way I know they are handled with TLC.

As an aside, when you carry a computer in luggage with wheels, do not roll the suitcase over bumpy terrain. It will jar the computer. Pick up the bag and carry it over rough surfaces, stairs and curbs. While this may seem obvious, it's easy to get caught up in the hustle and bustle of travel, and get lax about the computer bag. Become obsessive about that bag. It contains your lifeline to work.

You may wonder if a cordless phone, headset and answering machine are worth the additional bulk and weight they add to your luggage. The answer is maybe. First of all, only consider lightweight and compact equipment. I prefer a separate phone and answering device because I don't always need them both. For instance I don't need the answering machine in a hotel that has voice mail. The modular approach is much more flexible.

Secondly, even in a hotel with voice mail, the cordless phone will come in handy. Sometimes the only phone in the room is on a tiny nightstand in a dark corner. With the cordless phone, you can work from the little table by the window, or wherever else you like in the room. And as I said before, the headset (which takes up *no* space to speak of) saves your neck and leaves your hands free. If your work is phone intensive, bring the cordless phone and headset. Just connect the cordless phone's base to the hotel phone's auxiliary jack.

The answering machine is optional in many cases. However, the answering machine can be crucial when you stay in someone's home. If they have a second phone line (for their computer or fax), you might be able to set up your phone and answering machine on that line during your stay (take care though not to inconvenience your host). Your phone calls and messages will not interfere with their main line. And you can leave precisely the outgoing message that serves your needs.

If your host has only one line and an answering machine or voice mail, weigh your options carefully. If your host is gone all day and doesn't use the home phone much, there might be no objection to amending the outgoing message. It could say something like, "You have reached 734-0987. We cannot take your call right now. Please leave a message for Ward and June Host, or Beaver and Wally Guest, at the tone. Thanks for calling." This can be done in your voice, or your host's, depending on your *host's* preference. Of course, you must remember to return the message to its original content when you leave.

Sometimes it is not appropriate to impose on a host's phone line at all. You be the judge. At times, you can have complete confidence that your host will want you to make yourself at home with their phone line. Your parents probably fall into this category. They are so happy to have you visit that they roll out the red carpet. Still, it's best to err on the side of courtesy. If you feel that using their phone and changing their message would create the slightest imposition, seek another route.

"Another route" includes using your cell phone. If you plan to use your cell phone, you won't need the cordless phone and answering machine. However, I have found that on long, phone-intensive trips, cell phones are still a little unreliable. They drop calls and get sketchy or no service in many residential areas.

A cordless phone and answering machine are ideal for reliability, but are more intrusive than a cell phone. Unfortunately there is no single right answer. Read each situation as it comes. Invest in all the equipment you need, so that you have several options at hand.

I also like to carry my cordless phone because it is pre-programmed with the speed-dial numbers (*aka* memory dial) I use most often. My travel phone even has my calling card number and PIN on speed dial so that I can charge my calls quickly and easily. To prevent fraudulent use of your calling card, treat these numbers with care. It's best to program the calling sequence so it is split into two or more memory locations on your cordless phone. Unwelcome users are not likely to figure out the sequence if they were to try using your calling card fraudulently. As an added precaution, keep a close eye on that cordless phone as you carry it around.

Calling cards bring up another etiquette issue. Get your long distance calling card *before* you start traveling. Do not charge long distance calls to your host. Even if they insist that you can use their long distance, do not do it! Not even with parents! Always, always charge long distance calls to your calling card. Another place to use the calling card is from a hotel or motel — their phone rate is almost always a whole lot higher than your calling card rate. If you plug your cordless phone into the hotel phone, you can speed dial the calling card number and it will be convenient to use.

Invest in the nuts and bolts and the toolboxes. They are what give you the freedom to work and travel. They are your lifeline to the working world. Take care of them, and they will take care of you.

Divine Simplicity

Elizabeth Scott

***Simplicity** translates into clarity. It's about making things easy, choosing a singular path. We've all heard that knowledge is power. Well, knowledge is also simplicity. The more you know, the more clearly you see your choices, and the more decisively you can act. Decisiveness is the ultimate in simplicity and in power. Absorb the knowledge in the following chapters. They are designed to help you simplify your choices and eliminate the clutter in your life. Then you can gain better focus as you pursue your dreams.*

Elizabeth Scott

-14-

REFINE AS YOU GO
Efficiency, adaptability and thoughtfulness tame chaos on the road —

Once you have taken a few trips, you'll have your tools together and working for you. But you will continue to work out the kinks as you encounter new environments on the road, each with its own set of challenges. Your individuality will show up more and more from this point forward. Differences in lifestyle, personality and career choice lead to a vast array of travel scenarios. Everyone approaches and solves problems differently and has a unique working style. Each career choice requires unique solutions. I cannot offer solutions for every possible situation, but I can point out as many considerations as possible. It is up to you to be prepared and adaptable in your own inimitable style.

No matter how much you plan ahead, things sometimes go awry. Electronics won't cooperate. People won't cooperate. Sources for travel research are way out of date. The big job you bid on comes in just as you head for the airport on a pleasure trip. It's good ol' Murphy's law.

Be prepared, like a Boy Scout. Boris the Boy Scout would do well to remember his scouting days: He was required to follow precise packing instructions before camping trips. Boris seems to have forgotten what he learned back then.

While Boris is a talented computer whiz, he's like a mad scientist. He is so involved in solving computer problems that everything around him goes to pieces. When he travels, he enters his motel room and unzips a torn duffel bag. It overflows with crumpled clothes, loose scraps of paper, tattered files and a leaking tube of toothpaste. Luckily the laptop is in a separate computer bag.

It's fortunate for Boris the Boy Scout that he has saved so many clients with his computer solutions. They are willing to overlook the disorganization, and his business carries on. Picture Boris as he settles into his Toronto, Canada, motel room at eight o'clock on a Thursday night. He has a client meeting early Friday morning. He needs to look over his notes before the meeting. Boris works best at night, so he seizes the moment to get his thoughts together. He pulls stuff from the duffel bag. Two shirts tossed to the right, pants to the left. He's tugging, pulling and pushing things around in the bag. "Where is that file? I know I put it in here!" He is getting nervous. There are two piles of clothes, papers and toiletries on the floor. He picks up his black leather jacket and sees it's smeared with toothpaste. "I'll deal with that later," he mutters.

Finally, he finds the file, scrunched up in the bag next to his shoes. The file is a mess, having been tossed about as the duffel was handled. Pages slipped out and are wrinkled and torn, but still readable.

Boris burns the midnight oil. He gets to the crucial part of his presentation and needs the specifications for the new system he will recommend. "Where are those specs? Aw, ma-a-an!" Back through the bundles of stuff on the floor, piece by piece. "Can't find the specs. Got to keep looking." He sifts and sorts some more. This is obviously going to take awhile.

Half an hour later, after sorting and rearranging the piles five times, Boris still hasn't found the specs. He decides to set up his laptop and see if he saved a copy of the specifications on a disk. He pulls the laptop out of his case and there is a piece of paper underneath. "The specs!" He does some calculations and edits his notes. He has refined the project to perfection and finished preparing for the meeting. The mad scientist in Boris came out. Outside the sun is rising over the cityscape. Time to shower and get ready to go.

It takes Boris an hour to find the right clothes, shake out the wrinkles, assemble his shower supplies, and pull himself together, but he makes the meeting on time. The client is thrilled with the proposal. In his client's eyes, Boris the Boy Scout has saved the day. So it was a semi-happy ending.

Boris had planned to stay in Toronto for the weekend to see the sights. After his Thursday all-nighter and a full day of meetings Friday, he crashes for 12 hours and is groggy the rest of the weekend. He doesn't really get to enjoy Toronto.

Valuable time is lost to disorganization — time that could be used for work or play. Organize your things so you can put your finger on what you need when you need it. The time spent creating an effective travel system yields high dividends: Consider it an investment.

Components that keep you sane

Even if you are more organized than Boris the Boy Scout, you'll feel a little flustered when you travel. Everything is less predictable. At home you have a routine. Important tasks get handled because they are habits. You pay bills, go to work, make and keep appointments, and keep up with household chores. You can usually put your finger right on what's needed for the task at hand.

But on the road, each time you unpack, there is a new layout and a new spot to place everything. Suddenly you can't remember where you put the airplane tickets, the client file, or your dirty laundry. You know it's somewhere in your room, but where? Mundane tasks can take on huge proportions because of disorganization and panic when you can't find what you need.

It gets easier with practice. Here are some tips to keep you on track, starting with your travel briefcase. The travel briefcase is a separate bag from the business briefcase that you use while at home. The travel case is always packed with your business travel needs, ready to go at a moment's notice. You'll find another copy of "Organizing a Travel Briefcase" in Addendum VII. Photocopy the addendum and check off each item as you get your briefcase permanently packed, always ready for the road.

ORGANIZING A TRAVEL BRIEFCASE

- Create three files that stay in your travel briefcase.

1. "Bills and Banking." In this file keep deposit slips, bank-by-mail envelopes and your "Bills to Pay" list. As you get ready to travel, slip in upcoming bills and other banking info for the road.

2. "Filing and Phone Book." Store a permanent copy of your phone database in this file. It's also handy to print out your e-mail address book and file it here. Papers that you generate on the road, which must be taken home and filed, can go here until you get home. This includes paid bills, receipts for taxes, and anything else that would go back into your home files.

3. "Out of Town." This file holds stationery, stamps, user's manuals for your cell phone and other equipment, medical insurance information, and other documents you need when you hit the road. Just before you leave, put travel brochures, restaurant reviews, maps and other miscellaneous information about your destination in it. When you arrive at your destination, store your plane ticket, itinerary and passport in this file until you are ready to leave.

- Take time to make a "Bills to Pay" list. Refer to Chapter 12 pages 120-122, and Addendum IV. Keep it in your briefcase in the "Bills and Banking" file. I mention this again to emphasize its importance.

- At the risk of sounding repetitious, make a hard copy of personal and business phone numbers and addresses, even if you have them in an electronic organizer or your computer. You'll be glad you did.
- Include phone numbers for customer service and technical support for your electronic equipment in your database.
- Carry spare batteries in your travel briefcase for your electronic organizer and other important equipment.
- Keep floppy disks or rewritable CDs in your travel briefcase so you can always find them. Use them at home and in your travels to back up your work.
- Back up your computer work obsessively.
- Put all of the following in your travel briefcase: a travel calendar, business cards, pens and pencils, a mini-stapler, paper clips, small scissors, phone cords, cord coupler and a 2-in-1 adapter. Keep these items here at all times so you don't have to pack so many little things each time. Take the scissors out of your carry-on luggage if you are flying. Keep the paper clips in a small container like an Altoids tin or empty pill bottle. The phone gadgets can go in a resealable sandwich bag.
- All business files for each trip will be carried and stored in your travel briefcase so you can grab them in an instant.

This may sound like a lot of bulk for one briefcase, but each component is small, so the end result is surprisingly compact. Keep these essentials in one place and you'll have far less panic and much more peace on working trips.

Store your travel briefcase in a handy location at home. Some things in it are also useful at home. I keep mine right behind my computer. It's out of the way, but easy to reach. If I use something from the briefcase, I put it back as soon as I'm finished.

Packing light in the clothes department

When you add your business equipment to your luggage, you can easily end up with back-breaking poundage. Be very efficient planning your travel wardrobe to compensate for the extra business weight.

Some people carry obscene amounts of luggage when they travel. They pack clothes in every color under the sun and only wear half of what they pack. For a seven-day trip, Denise the Dilettante packs two huge suitcases, plus two carry on bags that are bursting at the seams.

At the airport, she checks her big suitcases at the front entrance. They slap "excessive weight" stickers on each bag to warn the handlers. Then she plops down in the nearest chair until boarding begins for her flight. Her carry-on luggage is so heavy that she is not motivated to move even for a cup of coffee.

Upon boarding, Denise the Dilettante tugs, pulls and drags her bags to her seat. She looks around beseechingly until someone takes pity on her and helps hoist the bigger bag into the overhead bin.

This is not a fun way to start a trip. If you aspire to travel more than Denise the Dilettante does, pare down what you pack. Tonnage gets discouraging after awhile. Travel lean and mean.

Streamline your clothing by streamlining your color scheme. The easiest way is to stick to neutrals, with splashes of color in accessories. When I say neutrals, I mean black, brown, navy, gray, beige, camel and white.

When packing, choose clothes in two contrasting neutral colors. That's it, only two. You can work in a little color with lively scarves or ties, jewelry, an umbrella or other accents. The rest is neutral. You'll only wear these clothes for a short time — not long enough to get tired of them.

Take only two pairs of shoes. One casual pair for walking and a slightly dressier pair. Both pairs should be the same neutral color. If you have a formal event on the trip, add one more pair of dress shoes, the same color.

Here is an example of efficient wardrobe planning using black and beige as the two contrasting, neutral colors: Pack two pairs of black shoes and one black belt. Pack one jacket, one sweater, two shirts (blouses) and two pants (and/or skirts). All of these pieces should be black or beige: They can be prints or solids, but black or beige. Women might pack one dress with the same color choices. Purse and briefcase will be black to coordinate with the shoes.

When you add what you wear on the plane (which will be black or beige) to this list, you have enough clothes for a week with mixing and matching. For a shorter two-or-three-day trip, you could pack even less: Substitute one item where I said two. This approach works for men and women.

If you are not a black and beige kind of person, substitute two other neutral colors where I have mentioned black and beige. You could pack chestnut brown shoes and belt, and combine them with navy. White is a difficult travel color because it shows dirt too easily — beige is a good color for warm weather and conceals spots more effectively. Try mixing beige with copper-brown or ivory for a change.

Are the neutrals too dull for you? Sticking with neutrals is the easiest way to streamline your travel wardrobe, but there is an alternative. It just takes more color savvy to get it right. Combine one neutral, such as brown, with compatible colors instead of another neutral. Brown can go well with turquoise, coral, certain yellows and forest green, for starters. Pack brown basics (shoes, belt, purse and pants). The rest can be made up of colored tops and accessories that look good with brown. This can be done, with as few pieces of clothing as the all-neutral scenario — just with more color contrast.

By re-combining your separates each day, you can avoid feeling repetitious. Let's look again at the black and beige scenario:

- Day one: On the plane, wear your black jeans with a black knit shirt, black belt and black shoes. Your look is monochromatic and sexy — frumpy sweats aren't necessary for comfort on planes. Perk it up with some gold jewelry. For men, a bold watch to match a gold or silver belt buckle would provide the right highlights. On a rainy day, wear a black coat and carry a red umbrella to add some zest. When the plane lands, if you have to race directly to an activity, you'll still look fresh and vibrant in black with strong accents.

- Day two: Send the black clothes to the hotel's laundry service. Pull out beige slacks and a beige-and-black patterned shirt. Wear them with the black shoes and belt.

- Day three: You are able to wear the beige pants again, as they are still presentable. This time wear a black, lightweight knit sweater and black shoes. Women can add a print scarf that includes black and beige.

- Day four: You have a business meeting that requires stepping up the dress code. Wear black slacks with a matching jacket, beige shirt and patterned tie that includes black and beige plus some color. Women would wear either a black skirt or pants with a jacket, or a dress, accompanied by a scarf or bold jewelry instead of a tie.

I think you get the idea: There are many possible combinations from a few well-chosen pieces of clothing that don't take up much space or weigh a ton.

Notice how often I mentioned knits. Knits usually travel well without wrinkling. Pack clothes made of fabrics that don't wrinkle easily, and your maintenance on the road will be minimized. Here's a test to do before packing:

Set out the garment you'd like to pack on your bed. Hold a part of it, *i.e.,* sleeve or pant leg, in the palm of your hand. Squeeze the fabric tightly in your hand for about three seconds. Let go and look at the fabric. A good knit, microfiber fabric, jacquard or denim will probably show little sign of having been scrunched. They are great fabrics for travel. Silk or linen could well be a wrinkled mess in only three seconds. Imagine what they'd look like after several hours folded in a suitcase.

Keeping on schedule and adapting

Routine habits fly out the window when you travel. Wake-up times are often different, and everything is a little off for the rest of the day. It's easy to forget to look at your appointment book when you are not in your usual office setting. Force yourself to check your appointments and tasks before you leave your room in the morning. And review it more often than usual during the day to keep yourself on track.

If your attempts to stay on schedule fail, as you mix work with play, you might miss an important meeting. That's bad business, not to mention embarrassing. This is a particular weak spot for me because I'm terribly absent-minded. I do my best to use discipline and organization to make up for it. When all else fails, and I miss an appointment, it takes some fast thinking to handle my error with tact.

One time when I was traveling, I had a phone meeting with a West Coast client set for 7:45 p.m. I was going to call him from my cell phone. At 7:15 that evening, I sat down in a nice restaurant in front of the fireplace and ordered a lovely glass of chardonnay. I glanced at my watch and mentioned to my boyfriend, John, that in 20 minutes I had to leave the room to make a call on my cell phone. I figured that between the two of us we wouldn't let the appointment slip by. John suggested a quiet place where I could make the call, and we continued out conversation. Two sips into the wine I had completely forgotten my phone appointment, as did John (so much for *that* backup plan).

We had a romantic dinner and the entire evening went by without a second thought of the appointment. The next morning I started working and gasped as I saw the missed call in my notes. A million thoughts raced through my mind. "What to do? What to do!"

I could have made an excuse about being stuck in traffic with no cell signal, or something else equally lame. But I believe it is important to maintain integrity, even when it is difficult. I called my client, apologized, and told him the whole story, including the glass of wine and glancing at my watch. He laughed out loud. He said he could imagine it happening to him. We rescheduled our conversation for that evening, same time. I promised not to have a glass of wine first.

It turned out to be one of the most productive phone meetings I'd ever had. We started with a few more chuckles at my expense, and I apologized a second time. We covered everything we needed to for business, and the conversation was especially open. The usual wall between people who have not met in person was dismantled by the humor of my error. I ended the conversation by thanking him for his flexibility, and he said he was happy to help.

Work and travel is like a free-form dance, with a lot of unpredictability. At the same time, every step you take must be in rhythm with those around you. You might miss a step here and there, like I did missing my phone appointment. If you dance true to form (with integrity), in the end you'll get back in synch.

Getting home without disaster

It's just as hard to keep your wits about you when packing to return home as when you leave for a journey — usually you are rushing for one reason or another. The knee-jerk reaction is to grab everything as fast as you can, stuff it into your luggage and race out the door. *Big* mistake.

I was in that kind of rush when I packed to return from a trip where I had attended some formal events. Even in my haste I packed carefully to keep everything in good shape. I thought everything was under control as I departed. While the plane ascended, I reclined in my seat and started to nod off. A jolt startled me upright as my mind flashed: "Did I pack my evening gowns? I must have. But I don't remember!" It was a long flight and I wouldn't find out until I got home — needless to say I was too nervous to sleep.

When I got home I opened my luggage immediately. No gowns — they were hanging on a door hook 2,000 miles away. I had wanted to pack them at the last minute so they'd suffer fewer wrinkles and forgot them in my hasty retreat.

No one I knew would be at the house where I had stayed. Panic set in until I thought to call my friend, Lisa, who lived near the house. I told her how to get in and she located the gowns. She used my Federal Express account to ship them to me, and the clothing arrived without a hitch. Mine was a happy ending but a lot of time and money was wasted because I was in a hurry.

The lesson I learned from that mistake was a simple one: *Always* allow time to go through every room you occupied during your stay. *Do not skimp on this.* Open every drawer, even if you *know* you emptied it. Look under the bed in case shoes or anything else was pushed underneath. Check every door hook and handle for hanging items. Look in every closet. Do this in every single room. As you walk out the door, glance back in case one of your suitcases got left behind. It happens!

I was lucky and my valuables were returned to me. But many travelers never recover forgotten items, or they get them back damaged. Best to learn this lesson the easy way, from my mistake instead of your own.

Practicing houseguest skills

In Chapter 12 "Take It on the Road" we looked at business etiquette when setting up to work in someone's office. It's equally important to be careful of the social etiquette of a houseguest. This takes practice. This is so important you should copy the "Houseguest Etiquette" list in Addendum VIII and review it from time to time. Add your own ideas as you think of new ways to express appreciation to your hosts.

HOUSEGUEST ETIQUETTE

Your attitude as a houseguest should always be "Give more than you get."

- Observe the household standard of neatness, and then be even neater.
- Place your toiletries under the bathroom sink, in a cupboard or a drawer, or back in your luggage when not in use. Even if your host is not using the same bathroom, it is jarring to him or her to see the mess.
- Keep your luggage in a compact area rather than scattered around the bedroom. If there is space, keep everything in the closet.
- Make the bed every morning before you leave your room.
- Respect your host's schedule. If your host sleeps late on weekends, and you are a rise-'n'-shine type, tread softly. Maybe even sneak out to breakfast, so there is no chance you'll disturb your slumbering host, and return with breakfast pastries for everyone. Any time of day, respect your host's schedule.
- If you are sleeping on a sofa bed in a living room, put everything back in its place first thing in the morning. Make your presence invisible. The sense of order will be more calming for both you and your host.
- Notice what foods and drinks are on hand and purchase a supply — more than will be consumed during your stay. Ask. You may get your host to tell you what's needed in the house. Replenish, and then some.
- Even if your host is not a neat-and-tidy sort, do your dishes as you use them. Never leave a dirty dish on a table, counter or in a sink.
- If your host is cooking a meal, help out. If your cooking

abilities are limited, set the table, clean up after the cook, or take out the garbage. Look around to see what else you can do to be helpful.

- After a meal in the house, clear the table and do the dishes, before the host gets a chance to rise from the table. Insist that they sit. Or, at the most, suggest they keep you company in the kitchen while you work.

- Arrive with a gift for your host if possible. I like to bring gifts that represent where I live. Locally produced foods like chocolates from a local chocolatier, cookies from my favorite bakery, or something I have made myself.

- If you can't bring a gift, be on the lookout during your stay for a gift they could use. Maybe their teakettle is ready for the trash, or they don't even have one. If they brew tea in a cup, a pretty teapot might be great. A coffee aficionado might like a special coffee gadget. Or, buy an attractive CD stand for a music buff.

- If gifts make you uncomfortable, take your host out to a nice dinner. Even if you give them a gift, take them out to a nice dinner.

- Launder your sheets and towels before you depart. Remake the bed. If your plane leaves early in the morning, do it while you are packing, or else arrange and pay for maid service.

- **Give more than you get!**

Look at your stay from the perspective of your host. Houseguests are an intrusion, even when the host is happy to see you. The easier you make it for your host, the happier everyone will be, and the more likely you'll be welcome to come again.

If your host wants to spend time with you and it is a workday, compromise. Tell your host about the "Two-Hour Rule." Plan together to take a two-hour break during the day. Think of something short-and-sweet to do together. Then get back to work. Also let your host know the "Two-Day Rule." Then take at least two full days off to play at the end of the workweek.

Before you tackle the role of houseguest in your travels, I strongly recommend that you become a host. Several times. Invite family and friends from afar. It will be great to see them. But more than that, I want you to observe how you react to the intrusion.

The host-houseguest relationship is a bit of a love-hate scenario: In your role as host, observe both the good and the bad. Notice the thoughtful gestures that strike a pleasant chord with you — add new ideas to your "good houseguest" list. On the flip side, notice houseguest habits that bug you. Make a mental note or jot them down. Each time an action (or inaction) strikes a note of discord, promise yourself you'll never do it when you are a houseguest.

Pay close attention to the duration of their stay. How long is too long? In a large home with separate guest quarters, it's easier to tolerate a long stay. In a one-bedroom apartment with a sofa bed, a long weekend can seem *really* long. Once you have had guests overstay their welcome, you'll be more sensitive and less likely to intrude on someone else for too long.

I have found the best houseguests are people who often entertain in their own homes. They follow the rules I outlined, and they know what it takes to make the experience pleasant for everyone. They give more than they get. They have seen slovenly, inconsiderate people ruin a good thing. Stay in tune: Entertain in your home often, and learn from the experiences.

-15-

THE CRITICAL CORNER
Naming names — the good, the bad and the ugly among office product manufacturers and service providers —

I'm going to name names in this chapter. In my stories I will share my value judgments about specific products and services. These opinions are based on my experiences and those of my many friends who "have work will travel." There are some rave reviews and some pretty bleak ones. Please remember that my experiences are limited. When you doubt what I say, do some research of your own. I happily defer to *Consumer Reports* magazine, *PC World* magazine and other resources you can dig up in the library. I'm no technical whiz.

It's actually because I'm no technical whiz that I felt compelled to write this book: If I can figure out how to take my work on the road, you can, too. But I digress. Back to the story.

I went to visit my friend Annabelle Artiste awhile back. She said I was welcome to work in her home, and she even had some basic equipment I could use. I set up in her spare room where there was a multi-function machine by Brother: It served as a fax, copier, printer and answering machine. Everything I needed was there. I thought I was in heaven as I downloaded the machine's software into my computer.

The Brother icon showed up on my desktop, and I thought I was home free. The machine printed out a test page without a hitch, spitting out hieroglyphic-like script. I printed a sample of the document I was going to fax. It worked fine. Then the machine started to hiccup. I couldn't get the document to fax. I reviewed the manual and the "help" menu on the computer program, and tried lots of techniques that did not solve the problem. I turned to Annabelle. She was helpless — remember she travels with only a cell phone — electronics are not her thing. She owns the machine, but rarely uses it.

Flipping back through the manual, I found the Technical Support phone number, and called them. I was put on hold by an automated answering system. Luckily I had my cordless phone and headset so my hands were free to work, and I could walk around while I waited. I sat down to a leisurely lunch with Annabelle, then unpacked the rest of the files I needed for the day's work. The whole time the cordless phone was clipped to my hip and the headset was on my head, so I'd hear the technician come on the line. Suddenly, "clic-k," the connection dropped. I looked down at my watch: I had been on hold one whole hour!

I needed to fax that document, so I called back. I re-dialed and was put on hold: I got on my computer and began typing reports that needed to be finished by the end of the day. I used my time constructively and finished the reports, listening to the Muzak on the other end of the line. Then, "clic-k," disconnected again. It had been 45 minutes. "This is ridiculous. I give up!"

Off to the local copy shop I traipsed, fuming all the way, to fax the document. By the time I returned to the house, I was cooled off enough to enjoy the rest of the evening with Annabelle.

The next day I wondered, "Should I try Brother's technical support again?" Since I needed the machine the rest of the week, I opted to give it another shot. Maybe they were having a bad day yesterday. I dialed the number and got the cordless phone comfortably situated since it might be attached to me for awhile.

And sure enough, I was on hold another 45 minutes, performing little tasks while I waited. But, *finally*, someone answered.

I explained the problem. The phone rep connected me to a technician who sounded reasonably competent. It took us awhile to diagnose the problem and finally un-install, then re-install the software. But it worked. And he stuck with me through a long session.

The Brother machine Annabelle has is a good little machine, for the price. But I'd sure hate to go through that whole process every time I needed help.

The lesson? Check into the quality of customer support you are likely to encounter before you buy an important piece of equipment. Some manufacturers provide even less support than Brother did. There might be no contact number or e-mail address at all. Product reviews in magazines will often rate customer support. Pay close attention.

I can name two companies whose customer service and technical support deserve high marks: Compaq Computers and Dell Computers. I am sure there are other computer companies that deserve accolades, too. But these are the ones I know. Your computer is a finely tuned machine, and you'll need professional support for as long as you own it. Ongoing support is crucial. This is especially true when you travel a lot. If all things were equal, or even a little less than equal, between one of these computers and a brand whose quality of service was unknown, I'd choose Dell or Compaq. They both usually give one year of free technical assistance on most models, then a nominal charge for help thereafter. Their support tends to be accessible, competent, helpful and friendly. Shop and compare.

I have also experimented with live chat customer support on the Internet. Provided your problem still allows you to access the Internet, this is an interesting way to troubleshoot. For a long time I avoided Internet customer service because I wanted to hear a live voice. Live chat is almost as good, and it's actually fun. I logged onto the site and posed my question. In a few seconds, I got a response from a technician who politely introduced himself (we'll call him Harry the Hero). We typed back and forth, almost as seamlessly as a verbal conversation. He had me try some things, and we poked and probed. Harry finally figured out the problem and e-mailed me a detailed, step-by-step solution that was easy to follow once he and I logged off.

More computer companies and Internet service providers are encouraging customers to seek online support: It must be more cost effective for them. Let's face it, customer service is not a moneymaker for companies. Sales departments *make* money for a company. Customer service departments *cost* money for a company. They need to be run cost-effectively to stay afloat. If they are encouraging the use of online support to contain their costs, I am happy to oblige. It's kind of fun!

In the Internet world, as with computers and peripherals, all tech support is not created equal. Which reminds me of another story:

I was traveling once with a group of friends that included Jake the Jock. He's a great athlete and a great businessman but, as I alluded before, he'll never be mistaken for a technical guru. We arrived at a beautiful town in the mountains with plans to hike, mountain bike and visit with friends. This was a three-week adventure so we both brought our work. I offered to let Jake use my computer to check his e-mail while we were there.

He refused to try to start the computer, but would use it after I logged on for him. We had different Internet Service Providers (ISPs), so we poked and probed, but could find no way to get him into AOL, his ISP. I called my MSN technical support phone number for suggestions. They could not help me with another ISP. I could understand that, but it was worth a try. Jake the Jock didn't have a technical support phone number for AOL, so he called a fellow AOL user he knows, and found out how to get into AOL from my machine. Good deal. He got his e-mail.

The next day Jake tried to log onto AOL again, but something was wrong. Yesterday's technique didn't work today. He couldn't reach his friend and he threw his hands in the air. Had he brought the technical support number, he could have made a quick call. But he didn't want to dig deeper to find AOL's contact info. He gave up on the computer and his e-mail piled up for several weeks until he got home.

What's the message here? First, get products and services with reliable, *accessible* customer support. Second, enter your tech support numbers into your database where they are easy to find. AOL may have good support. I don't know because Jake didn't use it.

But there is another, more subtle lesson, I don't want to overlook. When I called MSN and was basically told "It's not my job," it was déjà vu. MSN has told me that before, more than once (in one form or another). They have another good one: "This call is going beyond my time limit. I'll have to give you the instructions and you can try it on your own. We are only allowed X minutes per call." And then, "You can call back again if the solution I give you doesn't work."

If it were a one-time incident, I'd chalk it up to one technician's error in judgment. But on three separate occasions I have been told that they cannot wait for their solution to download on my computer. So no one was there to help me test or do any additional tweaking. I was left hanging out to dry. I understand that customer support needs to stay lean and mean and cost efficient. But calls should not be handled this way. Even more frequently MSN has told me to call another technical support (like Internet Explorer), who turns around and tells me that only MSN can help me with the problem. Again, I'm stuck in a vicious cycle of nobody willing to take responsibility.

Before I got MSN Internet service I had Earthlink. The customer support there was far superior: like night vs. day. If the first-tier technician could not help me, I was immediately transferred to a more experienced second-level person. I could sense the competence through the phone line. A few times, when I was having problems transferring Earthlink to my new computer, things got very difficult. I was then transferred to a third-tier guy, a guru, and he would hang in there with me until the problem was solved.

As an Earthlink customer, I switched to MSN with reluctance. At the time, I could cut my Internet cost almost 40% by subscribing to MSN through Costco (a deal no longer available). I went for the money savings. In all fairness to MSN, there have been good tech support experiences, too. They are accessible and great at solving routine problems. Just don't take anything complex to them — they will refer you to your computer manufacturer's or your browser's tech support.

There is another AOL problem for Jake the Jock. While it is user-friendly for Jake and other inexperienced users, it has drawbacks. One of them is that Jake is not able to open e-mail attachments from people who are not on AOL. He gets furious when one of his friends with a great sense of humor e-mails him jokes that he can't open. Diana the Domestic Goddess has the same problem with AOL, so I figure it's not just Jake refusing to make a little effort. This is not a huge deal, unless your business will require that you open attachments from non-AOL users. If you are a technical whiz, you may have found a way around this little snafu.

By the way, AOL floods users with ads every time they log on. This drives Jake the Jock nuts! Until he clicks on each ad and sends a "No Thanks" response, Jake can't get to the information he actually wants. When choosing an ISP, bear this inconvenience in mind. It doesn't go away.

I have mentioned a few stores where you can buy equipment and ISP service. Now I'd like to elaborate a little. I always check out discount warehouses like Costco and Sam's Club first, because of their low prices, but I don't buy the first thing I see because their selections are limited.

Next I go to computer and office supply stores like Office Max, Best Buy, Good Guys and/or CompUSA. Office products are expensive and important, so I shop several stores and gather information. When you see a model you like, write down the brand name, model number, desirable features and price. This way you'll be able to compare products using your notes. You may think you'll remember, but all the product prices and features will quickly become confused in your head.

I tend to solve problems independently (with a little help from my friends in tech support), so I don't need to buy from a non-discount, specialty store. But if your experience is limited, and you have no techno-nerd pal to give you guidance, go for the first-rate sales support and service. This can include in-home installation. Skip the discount stores I mentioned and go straight to a specialty store that sells the products you seek. For example, Gateway Computers has storefronts that deliver top-notch service, and their sales staff takes the time to educate novice buyers.

Specialty stores' prices are often a little higher (though not always), but they give personalized service and take the time to thoroughly educate you before you buy. Check the Yellow Pages under "computers" or whatever type of product you want to buy. If the first place you go tries to rush you through the sales process, leave. Check out another store. Many technical sales people will help you make an informed choice, so hold out for a soft sales pitch. Specialty stores offer much more post-purchase support than discount stores.

I know of one discount store that is an exception to this rule: Best Buy stores often have a technical service desk in the store. My experience has been that their technicians are knowledgeable and want to help. When you select a product, ask if you get a period of free in-store technical service.

If you buy a computer in one of the chain stores, shop Internet services at the same time. Some of the chain stores have special deals on Internet service if you buy your computer in their store. Check it out.

Two computer manufacturers I know of — Dell and Gateway — have very good phone-order and delivery systems for the purchase of well-priced, custom-made computers. With a few exceptions, they steer clear of storefronts and large sales overhead. This frees them to concentrate on quality products, sales and service. It's all done over the phone (or the Internet). If you know what features and software you want, call and they'll assemble your computer to your specifications at a very competitive price. In a short time, they ship it right to your door. If you are a novice, I hear they are excellent at walking you through the process and helping you decide what will work for you.

As I mentioned before, Gateway also has storefronts now. So if you need to look and touch before you buy, go in and see what they have.

Dell is known for its superior customer service after the sale. This goes beyond the opinions of my friends and me. I've read many reviews that rate Dell tops in customer service (products, too). Give either one of these companies a call, and see if you feel confident buying over the phone. Everyone I know who has done it has been a happy customer.

Getting back to phones, I want to emphasize the importance of a quality cell phone and service. It will make all the difference in how well your cell phone serves you. The discount stores I mentioned usually sell a name-brand cellular service along with their line of cell phones. Do your homework with *Consumer Reports* and other resources. Find the stores that sell the highly rated brand you like. Right now Nokia tends to top the charts, but do fresh research, as this could change. It's a very competitive field: Ericsson and Motorola are always vying in the background for the top spot.

Compare cellular services at each store that carries your phone brand of choice. I have been very happy with AT&T. They even have their own little storefronts where they sell the Nokia phones I like. AT&T's sales people are knowledgeable and helpful. They even pulled out maps so I could see their geographic service coverage.

I have put both AT&T and Nokia to the customer service test on more than one occasion. They have very accessible customer service. And once connected, their reps are eager to please.

When I'm on the road and dial 611 for cellular customer service (at no charge to me), I'm rarely on hold for more than two minutes. However, if you are traveling in an area where another cell service dominates, 611 will dial you into *that* service instead of your own. Use the toll-free number for customer service (a free call from your cell phone), to access your own cellular support when outside your area or from a land phone. Enter that number into your cell phone memory dial program, as well as your phone book database.

I know people with other brands of cell phones and cell services that suffer dropped calls right and left, plus poor sound quality — and they might be sitting right next to me while I am having *lengthy*, uninterrupted conversations with my Nokia phone and AT&T service. So I know that all products and services are not created equal. I have converted more than one friend.

If you do not have access to Nokia or AT&T, ask around. You'll probably find someone who is as enthusiastic about his or her cellular system as I am about mine. Follow up with that, and do further research before acting.

With any cellular phone service, choose your billing plan wisely. Most cellular services allow you to adjust your billing plan as often as you need, at no extra charge, until your phone plan most closely matches your actual usage.

Let's say you select a fixed-rate plan, where you get 480 minutes (eight hours) for $40 a month, and the minutes are good anywhere in the United States, 24 hours, seven days a week. Watch your actual usage to see if you have a close match. Say you pay 25 cents per minute for the time you use above the 480 minutes. After monitoring your actual usage for a couple of months, you might want to revise your billing plan. For example, if you seldom go out of state and you are using more like 560 minutes a month, you'd better change your plan. Those extra 80 minutes cost you $20 a month, so you are paying $60 a month for your cellular usage, and you are paying for an out-of-state-option you don't need.

You could call 611 or the toll free number and ask them to change you to a program that would assess roaming charges out of state and give you more minutes. You don't call out of state anyway, so the roaming charges won't hurt. You might be able to get the new package for $20 or $30 per month. You'd be using the phone the same way as before, but paying up to $40 less for the service. Your $40 monthly savings adds up to $480 a year. You could buy a pretty nice combination printer-fax-scanner-copy machine with the savings. Or, how about a round trip plane ticket to your next dream destination?

Buy a cell phone model that includes a call counter. It counts the time you spend on the phone. At the beginning of every billing cycle, set the counter to zero. Monitor your usage as you go, making sure you don't go over your allotted monthly minutes. Change your plan mid-month if you are calling more than expected: Call 611 and increase the number of minutes you are allowed (for an increased flat fee). It's better to pay a higher flat rate than a high cents-per-minute charge for going overtime. On the other hand, reduce the number of minutes in your plan if you are not using the phone much. You'll save money. Most cellular services do not charge for these changes (check before you enroll). The call counting feature makes it easier to stay within your cell phone budget. It's an important feature to shop for.

Call counters on cell phones count actual minutes used. Since most cellular services round up to the next higher minute after you hang up, your bill will not agree with the counter. If your call counter shows 5 minutes and 12 seconds on your last call, you may be charged for 6 minutes. Add an extra 25 percent to 33 percent to the number of minutes on your call counter — that will more closely reflect your actual cell phone bill.

With regard to regular land phones, there is a huge disparity between services. I spend a lot of time in three states, and have drastically different experiences in each state. When I lived in California, I used Pacific Bell. I took their efficient customer service for granted until I moved to Arizona and had to use Qwest. I have set up several phone lines on three different occasions with Qwest.

I now get out a legal pad and take notes during every conversation with the company.

I have written up to six legal-sized pages of notes (and my handwriting is small) to get one phone line properly hooked up with the right amenities. Each time I call them I write down the rep's name, date and time of the call, and every bit of our conversation including the promised solution. They have never gotten it right on the first, second or third try. They often don't have a record of my service request. I have been referred to other departments with different phone numbers in other regions. When I reach them they have no idea what has transpired to that point, and no way to find out. One hand definitely does not know what the other hand is doing here.

My experience with Qwest is not isolated. I have spoken with many people who have been left in limbo with their phone service: They tick off each offense on their fingers, as they describe their attempts to get it to work with Qwest. How does Qwest stay in business?

We don't have much choice in the phone service provided in each geographic area. Despite their virtual monopolies, we can be proactive. If you have recurrent nightmares with your telephone provider, take detailed notes as you go. Write down names, dates, times of day and what was said. Then contact your state's Public Utilities Commission, or the Corporation Commission, or an equivalent watchdog group. You can either file a report with them, or they can tell you who to go to for immediate results. Phone companies and other utilities *hate* to have these kinds of filings against them. State commissions keep track of these complaints, with dire consequences for the utility if the complaints are too numerous.

Jake the Jock is impatient with such foibles and has pursued this course of action before. He filed a complaint with his state's utility watchdog when his phone company's bad service got out of hand. The day after his report was received, the problem was immediately and miraculously solved, and the phone company continued to follow up with him to make sure he stayed happy.

Also remember that your basic phone service and your long distance service can be handled separately. You need not pay the (usually) higher long distance rates charged by the phone company. Check out independent long distance carriers. These service companies make it very easy to change. It's usually a one-step process. The cost savings are worth the nominal effort.

-16-

LEAP OVER THE PITFALLS
Bridge potential problems of combining work and play —

Remember how long it took me to get ready to work at Annabelle Artiste's house? That fax machine took hours to set up because of technical problems. No one is immune to these setbacks. When you travel, allow extra time for the initial setup of your workspace.

It takes awhile to find electrical outlets and phone jacks, the best light, and the best table or desk space. You have to determine what extension cords and other adaptations are needed to make everything functional. Still, after that, you must test your equipment after it is set up. Even if your first test run is a success, the whole setup takes time, so plan for it.

Sometimes when you travel you'll have a nice office in your host's home. Other times you will sit on a motel bed, talking on the phone and taking notes on the nightstand — your workstation competing for dominance with your sleepspace and anyone else in the room who might want to sleep or watch TV. Or you might work on the kitchen table in someone's home, which means clearing your work from the table every time people want to eat. Or perhaps you're in a house, working in an open alcove next to the living room, where five of your pals are gabbing up a storm.

There are a couple of "mantras" you can chant to yourself in awkward times. One is, "I am creative and will come up with a solution to this work situation. And I will handle everyone involved with tact." The other is, "I am lucky enough to travel to this special destination. I will happily work around any inconveniences." Think positive. A solution will come.

One winter, I was in a three-level ski home with five other people. At first I set up work in the loft overlooking the living room. It was fine during the day while everyone was downhill skiing. But early in the morning or late in the day, it was noisy with everyone around. I felt guilty asking people to be quiet when I was on the phone.

I unhooked all my equipment and dragged it to the ground-level spare bedroom. I carried down my files and laid them out again. The effort was worth the uninterrupted silence. There wasn't a desk in the room, so I took a 2-by-2 foot square of Formica I found in a closet and set it on the bed (a wooden cutting board would also work). It turned the bed into a firm writing surface where I could work. The laptop computer was plugged in nearby on an overstuffed chair — a funky setup, for sure, but it worked just fine for a week.

And don't worry that I didn't have any fun. I went cross-country skiing every day — getting my daily fix of pristine snow and an hour of rigorous exercise while gliding along riverbeds and through forests. I was quite happy with that daily adventure, and in the evenings I relaxed and enjoyed my friends.

Darrel the Devil's Advocate has done me one better in the creative workstation department: In nice weather, if the house or hotel is noisy, he takes his cell phone, notepad, pen and daytimer out onto the deck. He's taking care of business as he basks in the sun.

It is almost always more expensive to work from a travel destination. Most cellular plans are more expensive per minute than traditional long distance. When you are away, you use your cell phone more, so phone bills tend to be higher during that time. Obvious travel expenses like lodging, car rental, eating out and entertainment make the comparison to staying at home no contest. It's much more expensive to travel in most cases.

Don't get discouraged. There are ways around this. Remember the mantra, "I am lucky enough to travel to this special destination. I will happily work around any inconveniences." Get creative. Your first travel adventures could be road trips in your own car, and you could stay with family and friends. Then your only extraordinary expenses are for gas, host gifts and meals out. Or rent a large vacation home with a group of friends. Share the expenses. Don't go to the most expensive restaurants. Find the fun little cafes that are unique to the area. You get more local flavor in the small, quaint places anyway.

Over time, as you build your "have work will travel" business, your income will increase (at least that's the idea). Have a savings plan for trips that cost more. Don't take a trip until you can pay cash for your travels. At first, stick to domestic travel. It is usually much cheaper than foreign travel, though I've had some pretty inexpensive and memorable journeys in Mexico and Canada.

When you are ready for foreign travel, plan a house exchange. This way your only major expense will be airfare since there'll be no housing expense. Review Chapter 8 if you think you want to pursue this option. Or, get some friends to go with you and share the lodging expense.

My own foreign travel, which I do one or two times a year, is my "real" vacation time. I don't bring any work or even my cell phone. Telephone costs can be astronomical from other countries, and some foreign phone systems are quite inconvenient to use. The Internet is the only inexpensive, convenient form of communication from most foreign countries. So, that's my time off. Overseas travel is pure vacation for me. However, every time I travel domestically on weekdays, I bring my work with me to remain accessible to clients. Christmas is the only domestic trip I take when I do not work.

While I am on a real vacation, I leave an outgoing voice message that says, "You've reached Elizabeth. I am away from the office until [insert day and date]. Please leave a message and I will return your call at that time. Thanks for calling." That way I have no guilt while I am gone. People know not to expect a return call right away.

At this point, you may still have a nagging worry: "OK. It costs more to travel, and I work fewer hours when I travel because of the 'Two-Hour Rule' and travel time. So how do I earn enough to stay afloat financially, and take trips, too?"

It is easier than it might seem. For one thing, hour for hour, independent contractors often make quite a bit more than they would working as someone's employee. And, if you do the math in Chapters 8 and 9 (or Addenda I, II and III), you may find that you have fewer expenses. Apply some of the extra income, or savings from fewer expenses, to the cost of taking trips.

Another solution is to work overtime when you get back from a trip. The value I get from my travel experiences makes it infinitely worth the overtime I put in when I get home. Remember, "I am lucky enough to travel to this special destination. I will happily work around any inconveniences."

Many people who dream of working and traveling see it as an unattainable dream. My friend Winona the Worrywart is like that. She says, "I'd love to work and travel. What could I do that would give me enough money to get started? I couldn't give up my job and make enough. It's a shame; I'll never be able to do it." Part of the reason she sees her dream as unattainable is that her vision starts right off the bat with cruises and flights to New York City and Europe. No wonder she thinks, "It's just not for me." It hasn't occurred to her that she could take her work and visit her sister in Colorado. Or she could see her childhood girlfriend who moved to Oregon. And then there's her former co-worker and friend in San Francisco. These are all very special places. If she would think of the idea in baby steps, Winnie could do it.

Winnie has an excellent reputation as an escrow officer. Many of her loyal clients would love to have her do their bookkeeping. Before leaving her job, she could start the business on evenings and weekends, then build from there until she is confident she can support herself.

Winona the Worrywart's next concern is, "I could never give up my job. I get my medical insurance through work." Always an excuse with Winnie! If she looked at her insurance options at work, she would see that they include a Kaiser health plan. Kaiser will convert her group coverage to individual coverage, provided she submits her conversion paperwork within the required time limit after she leaves her job. No previous illnesses or injuries would exclude her. And the monthly premiums would be only a few dollars more than she now pays for group coverage on another plan. So, no excuses, Winnie!

Before you make the medical insurance excuse, review your employer's insurance options. See if you can convert one of the plans to long-term individual coverage after you leave. This has to be a commitment *beyond* the 18-month mandatory COBRA period. If it is not available after the COBRA period, apply for individual medical insurance elsewhere *before* you leave your employer. Make sure you qualify before you take the leap into self-employment. You might have to sacrifice certain coverage options like chiropractor, or even continuing with your current physician, to keep your premiums from skyrocketing. If you are married, see if you can be added to your spouse's health insurance at work. Usually it is easy to add a husband or wife to a group medical insurance policy. If you truly have the travel bug, you'll find a way around the medical insurance excuse.

Another potential pitfall of this lifestyle is travel burnout. Pace yourself. In your enthusiasm to explore this new way of living, it is easy to go overboard and travel too much. If you are on the road too much, your business will suffer. And you will run yourself into the ground trying to juggle so much chaos. Avoid burnout. Start slowly with short road trips. Build up to more involved travel as you work out the kinks of your travel system. With experience, you'll learn how much travel you can handle without causing pain and suffering in your work and home-life.

-17-

ON THE ROAD AGAIN

"Have Work Will Travel" continues to be a life-expanding journey and an attainable one —

Practice, practice! That's what it takes.

Does this life sound like all work and no play at this point? I hope not, because nothing could be further from the truth. Yes, it does take a lot of effort and patience over a long period of time to put together a "have work will travel" life. But look at the benefits to be had along the way.

You get to take your work to dream locations, set up shop and leave before you get bored. It even increases your appreciation of home. You can work in the mountains and look out on pine trees. Or, work by the ocean and listen to it roar. You can work in a beautiful city and view the skyline. How about a quaint country town where you can bring your fishing rod? The possibilities are endless. Where would you like to go?

Building and living a work-travel life can be a wonderful journey. There is the joy of meeting new people with different ways of looking at the world. And there is personal growth when you overcome an obstacle, be it a major life struggle or an electronics hurdle.

Does it all sound too complicated? I have to admit there are times when I get frustrated — times when my smooth travels are disrupted by bumps in the road. In fact, I get downright furious sometimes. I've been known to blast everyone around me when things don't go right. I am working on that: My short fuse is one of my life lessons. I am learning and practicing patience on my journeys. Even if I was at home 365 days a year, I'd have to learn to manage my temper. I choose to learn while I travel.

We all have life lessons. Traveling will not take us away from those lessons. If you think that "have work will travel" is an escape, think again. The challenges of the road will stir up your demons and make you look them in the eye. This is not a life for those who can't face their demons: It is a life for people brave enough to take them on.

When you encounter problems at the airport, in traffic, with travel mates or with machinery, notice your first reaction. You might see anger, helplessness, greed, envy, panic or some other destructive response. We all have our demons, but we can choose our behavior when they surface. When your demon rears its ugly head, you have a second or two before you react. Your response might be a communication, a physical action or simply inaction. Your behavior will tell you so much, as you either succumb to immaturity or conquer a demon and take the high road.

So, yes, it can get complicated. As you gain more experience running your independent business and taking it on the road, you'll experience fewer complications. And when they flare up, you'll handle them more easily. If you learn patience, humility, confidence, maturity, thoughtfulness or any other of a host of fine qualities, the complications are a small price to pay.

Pace yourself in these lessons, like you pace yourself by not booking too much travel. You probably won't conquer a demon the first time you face it. For instance, if you have been pessimistic all your life, it's not likely to go away in a flash.

Darrel the Devil's Advocate could practice being more optimistic. He might start by recognizing when negative thoughts overly influence his behavior. At first, he could simply let that be and just notice it. As Darrel becomes more aware of his pessimistic tendencies, he could try to change them. When he is tempted to nix a plan without looking at possible solutions, he could count to 20 before doing anything. Twenty seconds will seem like a long time, as a million negative thoughts race through his head. After the 20-second pause, he could practice saying, "Let me give it some thought." This would give him time to seclude himself and try to write down a solution for every objection he comes up with.

Over time, as Darrel the Devil's Advocate practices buying time before acting on his pessimism, he will develop the habit of looking at all his options rather than focusing only on what might go wrong. But it will take time.

I'm no psychologist. I don't claim to heal neuroses. Yet I honestly feel that we can consciously work on our demons. We can learn to deal with life from a new, refreshing perspective. I see the challenges of work and travel as an opportunity to deal with these issues constructively.

It all takes time and patience. "Anything worth having is worth waiting for." Ever notice how astute clichés really are? "Anything worth having is worth waiting for" probably began as a wise parent's calming response to an impatient child. But it was so good that everyone latched onto it. The saying became widely used and is now cliché. They are wise words that are so apt for "have work will travel."

The work-travel life is worth it. It is worth waiting for your business to build. It is worth working out the glitches in your travel setup. It is worth the challenge of facing down your demons. Take baby steps in all aspects of the journey. Each tiny step builds on the last. Reflect back on and celebrate every accomplishment you achieve on the road. Each one takes you closer to your vision.

You have the rest of your life to try to get it right. What's the rush?

As you become more adept at "have work will travel," be sure to allow several weeks of real vacation time each year. It is true that all year long you will be going to enjoyable places, but you will usually be dragging along your work, and the burdens that go with it. It is a fun, well-rounded lifestyle, but sometimes you need to completely let go of the burden of work and rejuvenate.

As I mentioned, make real vacations out of the trips where communications are nearly impossible. It may be in a wilderness area where there are no phones and no cellular reception, or in a foreign country or on a cruise where phone communication can be difficult and expensive. On these trips I get to really rest and recharge my batteries.

Even if you won't be going into the outback or to a foreign country anytime soon, take real vacations anyway. Choose times when you need to recharge. Or choose times when there will be so many people and fun things to do that you just want to zone out and play for awhile. Plan ahead to take a real vacation. I recommend two weeks a year, minimum, of vacation with no work and no cell phone. Take more if you can afford it.

If you want to experience new things and have an active vacation, don't wait until you're run down before you escape. If you wait until you are run down, your vacation will probably consist of sleeping and eating. That's OK if that's what you want, but if you want a more energetic getaway, go *before* you're burned out.

I may have already beaten the **Two-Hour Rule** and the **Two-Day Rule** into the ground, but I want to emphasize it again. When you travel and work, it is so important to recharge your batteries as you go. Two hours off each day, and two days (minimum) off each week for fun and adventure is crucial when you work and travel. You will resent your work if you are missing out on the fun part of your travels. It's always a matter of pacing yourself.

The most important thing to realize is that you can get there from here. Wherever your starting place may be, you can do it. If you dream of having work that will travel, just take the first step. In fact, if you have gotten through this book, you already have taken the first step. Your next baby step might be to read the book a second time and jot down each step you are inspired to take as you re-read the chapters. Photocopy every addendum and complete the tasks on them, one by one.

If your first attempt to start a business and take it on the road flops, don't complain about it and give up. Use what you learned from the experience and refine. Then climb back up on the horse and ride. The next time you encounter hitches remember what you've learned. Reflect, look at your notes, and try new strategies so you don't repeat your mistakes.

And don't blame others! Look at what you, and only you, could have done better in the situation. It gets easier every time. Always get back on the road again, and take the high road every time.

I shared some of my life story in the first few chapters to demonstrate that you truly can get here from there. If you are in the depths of grief, in the middle of a divorce, or feeling defeated by health problems or financial woes, I hope my story inspires you. It's about baby steps again. Rarely is there a miraculous, overnight transformation. Yet, with just a glimmer of confidence, an ounce of strength, you can push forward and the mountain will gradually shift. Even if your confidence and strength come and go, seize the moment when they are present.

Set small goals. They accumulate into great changes over

time. Keep the grand vision in the *back* of your mind, and the smaller goals and baby steps in the *front* of your mind. Take one step at a time. Then, instead of a sense of futility, you will feel confident that your next small goal can be achieved.

Enjoy the process. If you postpone happiness until you are able to traipse off to Europe on a whim, you might never be happy. Treasure the small successes in your business, as you jump each hurdle. Appreciate the simple trips you take in your own state. Every step along the way has its pleasures to relish.

Enjoy the process and time will pass so quickly. Before long you will look around and realize "I've done it!"

Addenda

ADDENDUM I

WORK SHEET
MONETARY SAVINGS AND COSTS

STEP 1. SAVINGS

Current work expenses that you would *no longer incur* if you stopped working at an employer's site:

Activity	Per Day	Work Days/Month		Savings/Month
Commute by car, bus etc.	$ _____	x _____	=	$ _____
Dry cleaning	$ _____	x _____	=	$ _____
Lunches out	$ _____	x _____	=	$ _____
Breakfasts out	$ _____	x _____	=	$ _____
Coffee & latte breaks	$ _____	x _____	=	$ _____
Fast-food dinners	$ _____	x _____	=	$ _____
Child care	$ _____	x _____	=	$ _____
Misc. payroll deductions	$ _____	x _____	=	$ _____
Other	$ _____	x _____	=	$ _____
Other	$ _____	x _____	=	$ _____

Can you sell an extra car? For how much?
Divide that number by 12 = $ _____
Add up all expenses in the "Savings/Month" row.
TOTAL SAVED = $ _____

STEP 2. EXPENDITURES

Estimate your costs to run a business from home and travel destinations. Include only the costs *above and beyond* your current situation:

Estimated Expense	Per Year		Per Month
Advertising	$_____	÷ 12 =	$_____
Accounting & tax preparation	$_____	÷ 12 =	$_____
Car and truck expense	$_____	÷ 12 =	$_____
Education	$_____	÷ 12 =	$_____
Equipment			
(computer, cell phone, fax, etc.)	$_____	÷ 12 =	$_____
Office expense	$_____	÷ 12 =	$_____
Insurance	$_____	÷ 12 =	$_____
Interest expense	$_____	÷ 12 =	$_____
Legal and professional services	$_____	÷ 12 =	$_____
Repairs and maintenance	$_____	÷ 12 =	$_____
Supplies	$_____	÷ 12 =	$_____
Licenses	$_____	÷ 12 =	$_____
Business travel	$_____	÷ 12 =	$_____
Meals and entertainment	$_____	÷ 12 =	$_____
Utilities			
(phone service, Internet fees, etc.)	$_____	÷ 12 =	$_____
Other	$_____	÷ 12 =	$_____
Other	$_____	÷ 12 =	$_____

Total estimated expenses in the Per Month column for:
                    TOTAL SPENT = $_____

STEP 3. TAX SAVINGS

Your TOTAL SPENT column roughly mirrors what your tax-deductible items would be working for yourself. There will be variations, so always consult a tax professional before making final decisions. But for now, we are just estimating. Next, we will find out your estimated tax savings from self-employment. Multiply your TOTAL SPENT (from Step 2 on page 181) by your estimated tax rate. If you are unsure of your tax rate, check with your tax consultant. Or, for the sake of this illustration, plug in 25% to get an idea. We are used to thinking of taxes in annual amounts. But since we are dealing with monthly amounts so far, let's continue to get a monthly tax savings. So:

TOTAL SPENT $_____ x ___ % = **TAX SAVINGS** of $_____ per mo.
   Your tax rate or 25%

STEP 4. SELF-EMPLOYMENT TAX (SOCIAL SECURITY)

Current self-employment tax is 15.3% of your net earnings (if under $7,075 per month). **This could change. Check with your tax advisor.** Estimate the gross income you expect to earn. From gross income subtract your TOTAL SPENT to get net earnings. Multiply net earnings by 15.3%, or the number provided by your tax advisor, to estimate your self-employment tax. Divide that by two, because when you are employed, your employer pays half. You then have an idea of how much *extra* Social Security and Medicare you'll contribute. It will look like this:

EST. GROSS INCOME per month: $ _____
  (your own estimate)

Minus: **TOTAL SPENT**   − _____
  (from page 181)

Equals: APPROX. NET EARNINGS   = _____

Times: SELF-EMPLOYMENT TAX RATE   x _____%
  (15.3% or % from tax advisor)

Equals: **TOTAL SELF-EMPLOYMENT TAX**   = _____

Divide by 2: **SELF-EMPLOYMENT TAX**   ÷ 2 = _____
  extra tax you pay if you are self-employed

STEP 5. TOTAL MONEY SAVED EACH MONTH

To get your end result, do the following math:

Enter:	**TOTAL SAVED**	= $_____	(page 180, step 1)
Minus:	**TOTAL SPENT**	– $_____	(page 181, step 2)
Plus:	**TAX SAVINGS**	+ $_____	(page 182, step 3)
Minus:	**SELF-EMPLOYMENT TAX**	– $_____	(page 183, step 4)
Equals:	**MONEY SAVED**	= $_____	each month you work for yourself

If you have a negative figure in the MONEY SAVED total, then it would cost you more to work at home/traveling than to stay in your current situation. Now is the time to review your figures. See where you can cut costs to make it work.

ADDENDUM II

WORK SHEET
TIME-WASTERS IN THE WORKPLACE

STEP 1.

Time-Waster Activity	Daily (In Minutes)	Days/Week (That You Work)	Weekly (In Minutes)	Converted to Hours (Per Week Wasted)
Commute (door-to-door, round trip)	_____ x	_____ =	_____ ÷ 60 min. =	_____ hrs.
Vanity (extra maintenance for skin, hair, face & clothing)	_____ x	_____ =	_____ ÷ 60 min. =	_____ hrs.
Office banter (be honest now)	_____ x	_____ =	_____ ÷ 60 min. =	_____ hrs.
Office meetings (the ones that didn't accomplish a thing)	_____ x	_____ =	_____ ÷ 60 min. =	_____ hrs.

Enter the total in the final space to get the hours per month you could save by working in a home-based travel situation

TOTAL HOURS _____
WASTED EACH WEEK

TOTAL HOURS x 4 = _____
WASTED EACH MONTH

STEP 2.

What hourly rate would you charge if you worked for yourself? Multiply that hourly rate by the TOTAL HOURS WASTED EACH WEEK (on this page, above.) This determines the monetary value of the time you'd save working and traveling vs. working in a traditional environment.

$_____ your hourly rate X _____ **HOURS WASTED** = _____**MONEY SAVED**
                                                         EACH MONTH   **EACH MONTH**
                                                                                       by applying time
                                                                                       more effectively

ADDENDUM III

WORK SHEET
THE GRAND TOTAL OF MONETARY SAVINGS
BY WORKING IN A NON-TRADITIONAL ENVIRONMENT

Now you can see the whole picture. There are two factors that decide whether you will save money by having work that will travel. One factor is actual monies saved, and the other factor is the value of time saved when you no longer work in a traditional environment. To come up with a single figure that represents the total you will:

Enter your final total from Step 5 on page 184, "Monetary Savings and Costs" Work Sheet:
>**MONEY SAVED:** $ _____

Add in your final total from page 186, the "Time-Wasters in the Workplace" Work Sheet:
>**MONEY SAVED EACH MONTH:** $ _____

This equals your total savings by working at home and traveling:
>**GRAND TOTAL:** $ _____

A positive GRAND TOTAL means that it will probably be cost effective for you to work at home or while traveling.

A negative GRAND TOTAL means that it might not be cost effective for you to make a change in your work situation. Don't give up. Go back and see where you can trim costs. Or think of ways to boost your income in your new situation.

ADDENDUM IV

BILLS TO PAY

PAY	DUE	COMPANY	ACCOUNT #	PHONE # ADDRESS	AMOUNT

QUARTERLY, SEMI-ANNUAL AND ANNUAL PAYMENTS

ADDENDUM V
TRAVEL LIST

Travel keys	❏❏❏❏❏❏	Turn off computer	❏❏❏❏❏❏
Airline ticket	❏❏❏❏❏❏	Set call following	❏❏❏❏❏❏
Itinerary	❏❏❏❏❏❏	Drapes closed	❏❏❏❏❏❏
Passport	❏❏❏❏❏❏	Set light timers	❏❏❏❏❏❏
Maps	❏❏❏❏❏❏	Heater off	❏❏❏❏❏❏
Cash, traveler's checks	❏❏❏❏❏❏	Garbage out	❏❏❏❏❏❏
		Water plants	❏❏❏❏❏❏
Daytimer	❏❏❏❏❏❏	Discard old food	❏❏❏❏❏❏
Cell phone	❏❏❏❏❏❏	Give travel #s to family	❏❏❏❏❏❏
Headset	❏❏❏❏❏❏		
Cell AC charger	❏❏❏❏❏❏		
Cell auto charger	❏❏❏❏❏❏	Casual clothes	❏❏❏❏❏❏
Laptop computer	❏❏❏❏❏❏	Business clothes	❏❏❏❏❏❏
Computer charger	❏❏❏❏❏❏	Lingerie	❏❏❏❏❏❏
Floppy disks/CDs	❏❏❏❏❏❏	Nylons	❏❏❏❏❏❏
Project files	❏❏❏❏❏❏	Underwear	❏❏❏❏❏❏
Pen, pencil, marker	❏❏❏❏❏❏	Socks	❏❏❏❏❏❏
Computer paper	❏❏❏❏❏❏	Nightgown, robe	❏❏❏❏❏❏
Answering machine	❏❏❏❏❏❏	Slippers	❏❏❏❏❏❏
Cordless phone	❏❏❏❏❏❏		
Headset	❏❏❏❏❏❏		
Fax/phone cords	❏❏❏❏❏❏	Umbrella	❏❏❏❏❏❏
Phone 2-in-1 adapter	❏❏❏❏❏❏	Gloves	❏❏❏❏❏❏
Phone cord coupler	❏❏❏❏❏❏	Hair clips	❏❏❏❏❏❏
Checkbook	❏❏❏❏❏❏	Day pack	❏❏❏❏❏❏
Calculator	❏❏❏❏❏❏	Gym clothes, shoes	❏❏❏❏❏❏
Apron	❏❏❏❏❏❏		
Recipes	❏❏❏❏❏❏		
Food bars	❏❏❏❏❏❏	Sunglasses	❏❏❏❏❏❏
Cosmetics case	❏❏❏❏❏❏	Swimsuit, goggles	❏❏❏❏❏❏
Prescriptions	❏❏❏❏❏❏	Sunscreen	❏❏❏❏❏❏
Vitamins	❏❏❏❏❏❏	Shaver	❏❏❏❏❏❏
Herbal supplements	❏❏❏❏❏❏		
Tums, eye drops	❏❏❏❏❏❏	Hair dryer	❏❏❏❏❏❏
		Fingernail polish	❏❏❏❏❏❏
		Polish remover pads	❏❏❏❏❏❏
Music CDs, tapes	❏❏❏❏❏❏		
Books, magazines	❏❏❏❏❏❏		
Camera, film	❏❏❏❏❏❏		
Notepad	❏❏❏❏❏❏		

Elizabeth Scott

SKIING:
Goggles ☐ ☐ ☐ ☐ ☐ ☐
Hat, muffler ☐ ☐ ☐ ☐ ☐ ☐
Gloves, liners ☐ ☐ ☐ ☐ ☐ ☐
Skis, poles ☐ ☐ ☐ ☐ ☐ ☐
Boots ☐ ☐ ☐ ☐ ☐ ☐
After ski boots ☐ ☐ ☐ ☐ ☐ ☐
Ski clothes ☐ ☐ ☐ ☐ ☐ ☐

HIKING:
Boots ☐ ☐ ☐ ☐ ☐ ☐
Sock liners ☐ ☐ ☐ ☐ ☐ ☐
Hiking socks ☐ ☐ ☐ ☐ ☐ ☐
Hiking pants ☐ ☐ ☐ ☐ ☐ ☐
Fleece jacket ☐ ☐ ☐ ☐ ☐ ☐
Water purification kit ☐ ☐ ☐ ☐ ☐ ☐
Water bottle ☐ ☐ ☐ ☐ ☐ ☐

SUMMER:
Visor ☐ ☐ ☐ ☐ ☐ ☐
Sun hat ☐ ☐ ☐ ☐ ☐ ☐
Snorkel equipment ☐ ☐ ☐ ☐ ☐ ☐

BICYCLING:
Helmet ☐ ☐ ☐ ☐ ☐ ☐
Cycling pants, top ☐ ☐ ☐ ☐ ☐ ☐
Windbreaker ☐ ☐ ☐ ☐ ☐ ☐

MOTORCYCLE:
Helmet ☐ ☐ ☐ ☐ ☐ ☐
Goggles ☐ ☐ ☐ ☐ ☐ ☐
Jacket ☐ ☐ ☐ ☐ ☐ ☐
Boots ☐ ☐ ☐ ☐ ☐ ☐
Rain gear ☐ ☐ ☐ ☐ ☐ ☐

ADDENDUM VI
World Traveler's Packing List

THE BASICS

- ❏ Cargo bag/suitcase
- ❏ Shoulder bag/daypack
- ❏ Luggage ID tags
- ❏ Personal/student ID & driver's license
- ❏ Wallet and cash
- ❏ Traveler's checks
- ❏ Passport, visa, and tourist card
- ❏ Money belt and passport carrier
- ❏ Tickets
- ❏ Credit and telephone cards
- ❏ Health insurance card
- ❏ Emergency contact information
- ❏ Address book
- ❏ Phrase books and guide books
- ❏ Maps
- ❏ _____
- ❏ _____

CLOTHING

- ❏ Rain gear or seasonal coat
- ❏ Comfortable walking shoes
- ❏ Dress shoes
- ❏ Athletic shoes
- ❏ Sandals
- ❏ Rubber thongs/slaps
- ❏ Sweater
- ❏ Shirts/blouses
- ❏ T-shirts
- ❏ Jeans
- ❏ Slacks
- ❏ Shorts
- ❏ Underwear
- ❏ Socks
- ❏ Seasonal hat
- ❏ Gloves/mittens
- ❏ Bandanna
- ❏ Belt
- ❏ Long underwear
- ❏ Swimsuit
- ❏ Pajamas or nightgown
- ❏ Bathrobe and slippers
- ❏ _____
- ❏ _____

For Women

- ❏ Dress
- ❏ Skirt
- ❏ Slip
- ❏ Stockings/tights
- ❏ _____
- ❏ _____

For Men

- ❏ Tie
- ❏ Belt/suspenders
- ❏ Tuxedo
- ❏ _____
- ❏ _____

PERSONAL

- ❏ Soap and container
- ❏ Toilet paper
- ❏ Medicines and prescriptions
- ❏ Vitamins
- ❏ Shampoo
- ❏ Comb and brush
- ❏ Toothbrush, toothpaste, and floss
- ❏ Lip balm and sun screen
- ❏ Small towel and washcloth
- ❏ Premoistened towelettes
- ❏ Deodorant
- ❏ Earplugs
- ❏ Hairdryer
- ❏ Hair spray/mousse
- ❏ Saline solution
- ❏ Extra pair of glasses/contacts & prescription
- ❏ Sunglasses
- ❏ Feminine hygiene products
- ❏ Make up
- ❏ Razor and blades
- ❏ Shaving cream
- ❏ Aftershave
- ❏ _____
- ❏ _____

For Children and Infants

- ❏ Diapers and diaper wipes
- ❏ Toys and books
- ❏ Formula
- ❏ Bottles, brushes, and accessories
- ❏ Night light
- ❏ _____
- ❏ _____

OTHER USEFUL ITEMS

- ❏ Dried fruit & healthful snacks
- ❏ Books and magazines
- ❏ Playing cards
- ❏ Notebook and pen
- ❏ Stationery, envelopes, and stamps
- ❏ Business cards
- ❏ Inflatable pillow
- ❏ Emergency space blanket
- ❏ Pocket hammock
- ❏ Coat hangers
- ❏ Nylon cord/clothes line
- ❏ Laundry soap
- ❏ Flat rubber drain plug
- ❏ Scrub brush
- ❏ Voltage adapter and plug adapters
- ❏ Batteries
- ❏ Binoculars
- ❏ Sheet bag for hostels
- ❏ Small flashlight
- ❏ Watch and alarm clock
- ❏ Video camera, camera, & film
- ❏ Travel iron or steamer
- ❏ Sewing kit with safety pins
- ❏ Umbrella
- ❏ Compass
- ❏ Safety pins
- ❏ Sealable plastic bags
- ❏ Rip-stop repair tape
- ❏ Combination lock
- ❏ Nylon duffel (folded)
- ❏ Small nylon bags
- ❏ _____
- ❏ _____
- ❏ _____

CAMPING EQUIPMENT

❑ Sleeping bag and pad
❑ Tent
❑ Ground cloth
❑ Water bottle/canteen
❑ Cup
❑ Fork and spoon
❑ Cook kit
❑ Stove and fuel
❑ Matches
❑ Insect repellent
❑ Small first aid kit
❑ First aid booklet
❑ Blister kit
❑ Water purification tablets
❑ Water filter
❑ Pocket knife with tools
❑ Pocket sharpening stone
❑ Snake bite kit
❑ Hiking boots
❑ _____
❑ _____

ADDITIONAL TRAVEL GEAR

❑ Pet food and toys
❑ Laptop computer
❑ Portable printer and scanner
❑ _____
❑ _____
❑ _____
❑ _____
❑ _____
❑ _____

ADDENDUM VII

ORGANIZING A TRAVEL BRIEFCASE

- Create three files that stay in your travel briefcase.
    1. "Bills and Banking." In this file keep deposit slips, bank-by-mail envelopes and your "Bills to Pay" list. As you get ready to travel, slip in upcoming bills and other banking info for the road.
    2. "Filing and Phone Book." Store a permanent copy of your phone database in this file. It's also handy to print out your e-mail address book and file it here. Papers that you generate on the road, which must be taken home and filed, can go here until you get home. This includes paid bills, receipts for taxes, and anything else that would go back into your home files.
    3. "Out of Town." This file holds stationery, stamps, user's manuals for your cell phone and other equipment, medical insurance information, and other documents you need when you hit the road. Just before you leave, put travel brochures, restaurant reviews, maps and other miscellaneous information about your destination in it. When you arrive at your destination, store your plane ticket, itinerary and passport in this file until you are ready to leave.

- Take time to make a "Bills to Pay" list. Refer to Chapter 12 pages 120-122, and Addendum IV. Keep it in your briefcase in the "Bills and Banking" file. I mention this again to emphasize its importance.

- At the risk of sounding repetitious, make a hard copy of personal and business phone numbers and addresses, even if you have them in an electronic organizer or your computer. You'll be glad you did.

• Include phone numbers for customer service and technical support for your electronic equipment in your database.

• Carry spare batteries in your travel briefcase for your electronic organizer and other important equipment.

• Keep floppy disks or rewritable CDs in your travel briefcase so you can always find them. Use them at home and in your travels to back up your work.

• Back up your computer work obsessively.

• Put all of the following in your travel briefcase: a travel calendar, business cards, pens and pencils, a mini-stapler, paper clips, small scissors, phone cords, cord coupler and a 2-in-1 adapter. Keep these items here at all times so you don't have to pack so many little things each time. Take the scissors out of your carry-on luggage if you are flying. Keep the paper clips in a small container like an Altoids tin or empty pill bottle. The phone gadgets can go in a resealable sandwich bag.

• All business files for each trip will be carried and stored in your travel briefcase so you can grab them in an instant.

ADDENDUM VIII

HOUSEGUEST ETIQUETTE

Your attitude as a houseguest should always be "Give more than you get."

- Observe the household standard of neatness, and then be even neater.
- Place your toiletries under the bathroom sink, in a cupboard or a drawer, or back in your luggage when not in use. Even if your host is not using the same bathroom, it is jarring to him or her to see the mess.
- Keep your luggage in a compact area rather than scattered around the bedroom. If there is space, keep everything in the closet.
- Make the bed every morning before you leave your room.
- Respect your host's schedule. If your host sleeps late on weekends, and you are a rise-'n'-shine type, tread softly. Maybe even sneak out to breakfast, so there is no chance you'll disturb your slumbering host, and return with breakfast pastries for everyone. Any time of day, respect your host's schedule.
- If you are sleeping on a sofa bed in a living room, put everything back in its place first thing in the morning. Make your presence invisible. The sense of order will be more calming for both you and your host.
- Notice what foods and drinks are on hand and purchase a supply — more than will be consumed during your stay. Ask. You may get your host to tell you what's needed in the house. Replenish, and then some.
- Even if your host is not a neat-and-tidy sort, do your dishes as you use them. Never leave a dirty dish on a table, counter or in

a sink.

- If your host is cooking a meal, help out. If your cooking abilities are limited, set the table, clean up after the cook, or take out the garbage. Look around to see what else you can do to be helpful.
- After a meal in the house, clear the table and do the dishes, before the host gets a chance to rise from the table. Insist that they sit. Or, at the most, suggest they keep you company in the kitchen while you work.
- Arrive with a gift for your host if possible. I like to bring gifts that represent where I live. Locally produced foods like chocolates from a local chocolatier, cookies from my favorite bakery, or something I have made myself.
- If you can't bring a gift, be on the lookout during your stay for a gift they could use. Maybe their teakettle is ready for the trash, or they don't even have one. If they brew tea in a cup, a pretty teapot might be great. A coffee aficionado might like a special coffee gadget. Or, buy an attractive CD stand for a music buff.
- If gifts make you uncomfortable, take your host out to a nice dinner. Even if you give them a gift, take them out to a nice dinner.
- Launder your sheets and towels before you depart. Remake the bed. If your plane leaves early in the morning, do it while you are packing, or else arrange and pay for maid service.
- **Give more than you get!**

Elizabeth Scott

ADDENDUM IX

RESOURCES

Acupuncture
American Academy of Acupuncture
(323) 937-5514
www.medicalacupuncture.org/
JDOWDEN@prodigy.net
4929 Wilshire Blvd. Ste 428
Los Angeles, CA 90010

Auction Site
eBay   www.ebay.com

Bill Pay Service, Online
United States Postal Service (USPS)
(888) 508-7627
www.usps.com/paymentservices.com
icustomercare@usps.com

Business Service Centers
Kinko's
(800) 2-KINKOS
www.kinkos.com
customerrelations@kinkos.com

Cell Phone Manufacturers
Ericsson   www.ericsson.com

Motorola   www.motorola.com

Nokia   www.nokia.com
(888) 665-4228

Cellular Service Provider
AT&T Wireless
(800) 888-7600
www.attws.com

Computer Fax Program
WinFaxPro
www.symantec.com
(800) 441-7234

Computer Manufacturers
Compaq www.compaq.com
(800) 888-0220

Dell   www.dell.com
(800) 374-9223

Gateway   www.gateway.com
(800) 846-4208

Death and Grieving
Compassionate Friends (support groups for bereaved parents)
(877) 969-0010
www.compassionatefriends.com

Elisabeth Kubler-Ross, MD
www.elisabethkublerross.com
Books:
On Death and Dying
The Wheel of Life

Rachel Naomi Remen, MD
www.rachelremen.com
Book:
Kitchen Table Wisdom

Financial Software
Quicken   www.quicken.com
(888) 246-8848

Elizabeth Scott

Group Travel Opportunities
REI Sports Stores
www.rei.com/travel
(800) 622-2236

Sierra Club
www.sierraclub.org
information@sierraclub.org
(415) 977-5500
85 Second St., 2nd Floor
San Francisco, CA 94105

Individual Medical Coverage
Cigna
www.cigna.com/consumer

Kaiser Permanente
www.kaiserpermanente.org

Internet Browser
Internet Explorer   (425) 635-7123
www.microsoft.com/windows

Internet Service Providers
AOL   www.aol.com
(888) 265-8003

Earthlink
www.earthlink.com
(800) 890-6356

MSN   www.msn.com
(800) 386-5550

Lupus Information
Arthritis Foundation
www.arthritis.org
(800) 283-7800
PO Box 4284
Atlanta, GA 30357-0669

Lupus Foundation
www.lupus.org
(800) 558-0121
1300 Piccard Drive, Ste 200
Rockville, MD 20850-4303

Motivation
Anthony Robbins
www.tonyrobbins.com
Books:
Awaken the Giant Within
Unlimited Power

Cynthia Kersey
(888) 867-8699
www.unstoppable.net
Book: *Unstoppable*

Oprah Winfrey
www.oprah.com
O, The Oprah Magazine
The Oprah Winfrey Show,
ABC TV

Phillip McGraw PhD
www.philmcgraw.com
P.O. Box 140143
Irving, TX 75014-0143

Phone Service
Pacific Bell
www.pacbell.com
(800) 310-BELL

Qwest Communications
www.qwest.com
(800) 996-2347 Sales

Product Articles and Reviews
Consumer Reports magazine
www.consumerreports.org
101 Truman Avenue
Yonkers, NY 10803

PC World magazine
www.pcworld.com
letters@pcworld.com
(415) 243-0500
501 Second St. #600
San Francisco, CA 94107

Stores
Best Buy
www.bestbuy.com/StoreLocator
(888) 237-8289

CompUSA   www.compusa.com
(800) COMPUSA

Costco   www.costco.com
(800) 774-2678

Gateway   www.gateway.com
(800) 846-4208

Good Guys
www.goodguys.com
(888) 937-7004

OfficeMax
www.officemax.com
(800) 283-7674

Radio Shack
www.radioshack.com

Sam's Club
www.samsclub.com
608 Southwest 8th St.
Bentonville, AR 72712

INDEX

A

acupuncture · 15, 17, 199
  magnetic acupuncture · 15
  magnets · 15, 35
alternative medicine · 17
Annabelle Artiste · 112-113, 154
answering machine · 103, 107, 132-133
AOL · *See* Internet
appointments and tasks · 147-149
auction sites · 102, 199

B

Bills to Pay · 120-122, 142-143
Boris the Boy Scout · 139-141
briefcase · 139-132, 142-144
  cosmetic case · 130
  files that stay in your travel briefcase · 142-143
  ORGANIZING A TRAVEL BRIEFCASE · 130-131, 142-144
business classes · 96-97
business plan · 68-69

C

call following · 105
call forwarding · 105
call waiting · 103, 105
caller ID · 103
camping · 117-118
cell phone · 104, 108, 116, 133-134, 162, 168
  call counter · 164
  Ericsson · 162, 199
  Motorola · 162, 199
  Nokia · 162-163, 199
cellular service · 104, 118, 162
  611 customer service number · 162-163
  AT&T · 162-163, 199
  billing plan · 163-164
  fixed-rate plan · 163
  reciprocal phone service · 109
  round up to the next higher minute · 164

Cerebral palsy · 8
childhood memories · 20-24
Cleo the Corporate Climber · 87-88
clothing · 144-147
   color scheme · 144-145
   fabrics that don't wrinkle easily · 147
   neutrals · 144-146
computer · 104
   Compaq · 154, 156, 161, 199
   cybercafes · 109
   Dell · 154, 156, 161, 199
   Gateway · 161, 199
Consumer Reports magazine · 103, 154, 162, 201
copy machine · 110
Cream · 12
   "I Feel Free" · 12
   Eric Clapton · 12
curiosity · 52, 55, 64
   definition · 41

D

Darrel the Devil's Advocate · 76-79, 168, 174-175
daytimers · 111
death
   grieving · 5-36, 177, 199
demons · *See* life lessons
Denise the Dilettante · 61-65, 144
desktop computer · 104
Diana the Domestic Goddess · 99-100, 159
diet experimentation · 17
discipline · 52-53, 55, 65
   definition · 95

E

Earthlink · *See* Internet
eBay · 101, 102, 199
electronic banking · 119-120
equipment · 68, 76, 102-106
   Brother · 154-156
Eric Clapton · 12
ESSENTIAL TOOLS OF THE TRADE · 103-105, 130-134

etiquette
　　become a host · 153
　　friend or associate's office · 117
　　houseguest · 150-153
　　social etiquette · 153

F
fax · 104, 115
　　computer fax program · 110
　　plain paper fax machine · 104, 110
　　software · 104, 117
　　machine · 104
foreign travel · 169
　　foreign countries · 109
Francine Frantic · 90-92
friend or family home · 116
fulfillment · 51-52, 55, 64
　　definition · 3

G
Gary Golfer · 87-88
goals · 19
ground zero · 30

H
Harry the Hero · 157
headset · 105, 106
health plan · *See* medical insurance
home workspace · 102-113
honesty · 99
　　honest with yourself · 60
　　integrity · 148-149
hotel · 114-115
house exchange · 68, 169
houseguest · *See* etiquette
HOUSEGUEST ETIQUETTE List · 151-152
hypnotherapy · 16, 36

I

independent reviews · 103
   office equipment · 103
integrity · *See* honesty
Internet · 116, 119, 161, 169
   AOL · 158-160, 200
   Earthlink · 159, 200
   Internet Explorer · 159, 200
   ISP · 157-160, 200
   MSN · 158-159, 200
   services · 119, 157-161
Internet banking services · 119-120, 199
IRS Tax Form 1040
   Schedule C · 69

J

jack-of-all-trades · 61
Jake the Jock · 118-120, 157-160, 165
Judy Judge · 88, 101

K

Kinko's · 109, 112

L

laptop · 104, 109, 117, 131
life lessons · 174
   demons · 16, 65, 174-175
lodging · 114-118
loneliness working on your own · 84-85
   book club · 85
   bridge club · 85
   classes · 85
   group travel · 85
   investment club · 85
   join a gym · 85
   neighborhood restaurant · 84
   volunteer · 84
long distance
   long distance carrier · 106
   service provider · 164-165

lupus · 10-36, 200
   Arthritis Foundation · 200
   Lupus Foundation · 200

M

mail box rental service · 111-113
   U.S. Postal facility · 111
mail forwarding · 111-113
mantras · 167-169, 170
medical insurance · 171-172
   Cigna · 200
   COBRA · 171
   Kaiser · 171, 200
medication
   lupus · 17
meditation · 16
memories
   adult · 24-28
   childhood · 20-24
Microsoft Works · 124
MOBILE COMPUTER SKILLS · 96
MONETARY SAVINGS AND COSTS · 72-76
   EXPENDITURES · 73
   TAX SAVINGS · 74
   TOTAL MONEY SAVED EACH MONTH · 76
motel · 114-115
Motivation · 200
MSN · *See* Internet
multi-function machines · 104-105, 154

N

networking · 97-98

O

Office in another city · 117

P

packing · 131-132, 144-147
Palm Pilots · 111
parenting · 85-86
PC World magazine · 154, 201
Pegasus · 24
Peripheral equipment that will travel · 110
Phone · 103
    calling cards · 106, 108, 109, 134
    cordless phone · 103, 105, 107, 132, 134, 155
    900 MHz (megahertz) · 106
    land phone · 164
    long distance · 106, 134, 166
    more phone concerns · 105-109
    outgoing message · 109, 133
    Pacific Bell · 164-165, 200
    phone accessories · 131, 143
    prorate the minutes · 106-107
    Qwest · 164-165, 200
    speed dial numbers · 108, 134
portable skills · 96
printer · 105, 117
    portable · 110
psychotherapy · 17

Q

Quicken · 119, 199
Quicken for Dummies · 96

R

real vacation · 169-170, 176
Reggie Real Estate · 88, 101
REI Sports Stores · 85, 200
relationship issues · 86-88
RESOURCES · 199-201
roommate · 114-115

S

self-education program · 97
self-employment tax · 69-70, 75
Sierra Club · 85, 200
simplicity · 53, 55, 63
   definition · 137
Social Security
   Disability Income (SDI) · 31-32
Social Security and Medicare withholdings ·
   See self-employment tax
socializing after work ·
   See loneliness working on your own
Special Olympics · 7
stores ·
   Best Buy · 160, 161, 201
   CompUSA · 160, 201
   Costco · 160, 201
   Gateway Computers · 159-160, 201
   Good Guys · 160, 201
   OfficeMax · 131, 160, 201
   Radio Shack · 131, 201
   Sam's Club · 160, 201
strengths · 56-59. 65

T

tax advisor, See taxes
tax deductible · See taxes
tax savings · See taxes
taxes · 67-70, 74
technical support · 155
   customer service · 156-159
   live chat · 156-157
telecommute · 98
test your current level of self-discipline · 97
time wasters · 80-83
   commute · 80
   office banter · 80, 84
   office meetings · 81
   vanity · 80
travel budget · 71
travel burnout · 172

travel list · 123-129
Two-Day Rule · 116, 153, 176
Two-Hour Rule · 116, 152, 176

U

United States Postal Service (USPS) · *See* electronic banking

V

Visors (PDAs) · 111
voice mail · 103, 105, 109, 115, 133

W

watchdog groups · 165-166
   Corporation Commission · 165
   Public Utilities Commission · 165
weaknesses · 56-59, 65
What Color Is Your Parachute? · 48
WinFaxPro · 104, 199
Winona the Worrywart · 170-171
WORK SHEET · 72-76, 82, 83, 121-122, 180-184, 185-187, 188
   MONETARY SAVINGS AND COSTS Work sheet · 72-75
   THE GRAND TOTAL OF MONETARY SAVINGS · 76
   TIME-WASTERS IN THE WORKPLACE · 82
WORK THAT FITS WITH TRAVEL List · 100
World Traveler's Packing List · 127-129

Y

youth hostels · 117-118

ABOUT THE AUTHOR

Elizabeth Scott

Elizabeth Scott is expert at turning traditional jobs into traveling jobs. But her life has not always been so free-spirited. She began her adult life as a college student and mother of two in California's wine country. Her second child was diagnosed, at one-year old, with severe brain damage. Elizabeth left school to care for her daughter, gaining far more education than college courses could have imparted.

She worked full time with her daughter's special needs and on disability advocacy; gradually phasing in her own career in banking. The stress of those years brought on what became a severe case of lupus. While Elizabeth was disabled and sidelined from banking, her daughter died at the age of eight years old.

Over many years Elizabeth rebuilt her life by applying lessons hard learned, and carving a life more true to her ideals. As she healed, she migrated from banking to real estate sales and investment, and then executive recruiting. She was also a television "home expert" on NBC news in San Francisco. For seven years she has taken work with her as she travels up to 50 percent of the time. She now blends her career as author of *Have Work Will Travel*, marketing consultant and speaker with her travels. She is innovative as she mixes work and play, living life to the fullest.

"I am a wanderer at heart. As I explore I find enriching experiences at every turn. These sojourns are only partially rich, until they are shared with others and made full. By sharing my story and how to 'have work will travel,' I hope that the reader becomes as enriched as I am in the telling of the story."

Elizabeth Scott is available to speak at seminars and events. She speaks on issues of surviving catastrophic loss, and how to create a *Have Work Will Travel* life. You can contact her at:

Elizabeth Scott
elizabeth-scott@excite.com
(877) 202-2540

ORDER AUTOGRAPHED COPIES

You may know someone who is bereaved, recovering from a serious illness or at a crossroad in their life with no idea where to turn. I would be honored if he or she found solace, inspiration or clarity from my words. You can share *Have Work Will Travel* with a family member, friend or co-worker and I will autograph your gift at no extra charge.

Discounts apply for 2 books or more:
1	$16.95
2	$15.95 each
3-4	$14.95 each
5-10	$12.95 each

Purchase *Have Work Will Travel* one of two ways:
1. E-mail elizabeth-scott@excite.com and provide the information requested below. You will receive a return e-mail with the total price including tax and shipping, and how to submit payment. OR:
2. Call **(877) 202-2540** and provide the following:
   - ✓ Your name (please spell)
   - ✓ Your phone number (speak slowly and clearly)
   - ✓ Your mailing address
   - ✓ Number of copies you are buying
   - ✓ The names of each gift recipient (please spell)

You will receive a phone call that explains total price with tax and shipping, and how to submit your payment.

Thank you,

Elizabeth

Elizabeth Scott